How Advertising Works

How Advertising Works

A review of current thinking

COLIN McDONALD

THE ADVERTISING ASSOCIATION
—— IN ASSOCIATION WITH ——
NTC PUBLICATIONS LTD

First published in 1992
Reprinted 1993
NTC Publications Limited
Farm Road
Henley-on-Thames
Oxfordshire RG9 1EJ
United Kingdom
Telephone: 0491 574671

A CIP catalogue record for this book is available
from the British Library

ISBN 1-870562-42-9

Typeset in 12/14pt Times
by NTC Publications Ltd
Printed and bound in Great Britain by
Biddles Ltd, Guildford and Kings Lynn

Contents

Contents

1 Introduction

'Advertising is being more and more widely regarded as an essential factor in modern commerce, and its successful practice must necessarily be founded on the acquisition of scientific knowledge over a wide field.'

(Introduction by the General Editor, The Library of Advertising, W. Henderson Pringle, 1932)

Few writers nowadays would have the effrontery to preface even a textbook on advertising with such a boast. The very idea that it was possible to 'acquire scientific knowledge over a wide field' in an area so varied and diffuse would be dismissed in many quarters with derision. We all know that it is not as simple as that. There is at least a strong school of thought which holds that, since all attempts to find a comprehensive theory have failed, it is a waste of time to try: advertising can only be guided by practical common sense, and every case is different.

Yet even those who hold this view would probably agree, if pushed, that, for all its variety, advertising does have some common features which distinguish it from other kinds of promotion. There may be no 'science of advertising', but we share an awareness, however vague, of what makes advertising different: we can see that advertisements for, say, a lavatory cleaner, a perfume, a motor bike, a unit trust and an injunction not to drink before driving are *like each other* in certain ways in which none of them is like a price cut or a special offer. If these features can be described and understood, it should help to clarify the rules and constraints under which advertising operates: what it can and cannot do, and what it does best. Guidelines for thinking productively about advertising, in any particular context, then become easier. To pull out these features that distinguish advertising, and look at them afresh, is the main purpose of this review.

Motivations for seeking an explanation of advertising

People have been looking for explanations of advertising for a long time. The search has been fuelled by a number of motivations:

- *The wish for professionalism*, so that the status and earning power of those who practise the art may be demonstrated, and passed on with proper training. One of the purposes of The Library of Advertising was stated as: 'the volumes will be of great practical utility in reading for the examinations which (the student) must pass before taking his place as a trained and competent member of his profession.'

- *Accountability*. The need for accountability becomes more urgent when costs rise and recession squeezes. ' The nineties ... will see increasing pressure for advertising money to work harder and be accountable.' (Feldwick[35]). It depends partly on what one means by 'accountable'; if the only criterion regarded as relevant is a quick increase in sales, which can be observed to follow a price cut or special offer more strikingly than an advertising burst, it must put the advertising budget in danger. It has to be shown that the purpose of advertising, and therefore what is to count as 'accountability' for it, ought not to be described in this way.

- *The continuing need for ammunition* to put the case against those who believe that curbing advertising is the best way to prevent some social evil. This kind of attack puts advertising in a particularly nasty double bind. If we deny that advertising is a potent force in spreading the undesirable habit, we seem to be open to the question: 'well then, what does it do?' Either advertising works,' so we should stop it, or it is ineffective, in which case why bother with it? Only a demonstration of what advertising actually does do can counter such an attack; and it must *be* a real demonstration, not wishful thinking.

With these motives, it is not surprising that people involved in the business should, from early days, have tried to find out the rules, not just for theoretical interest but to provide a practical means of assessment. But, as we all know by now, it has not proved so simple. There have been quite a number of plausible 'models', well presented with supporting evidence; but every one has run up against some situation or example which won't fit; none have proved universal. Every time we think we have caught the fish, it slips through our fingers. And this has helped to keep in being the negative school of thought that it is impossible to understand advertising objectively or, perhaps worse, that it is of no practical help to try. In paper after paper, right up to the present, one finds the refrain: 'we *still* do not understand (or, if only we understood more about) how advertising works.'

We know more than we think ... but not enough
This view is certainly too gloomy. There are good grounds for saying that we have made considerable progress in our understanding of advertising over the years. One reason is that the sheer effort of struggling with the difficulties gives us new insights: every time we have found a theory blocked, we have been forced to enlarge our vision as we try to get round it. Most of the theories are not completely wrong, but right for certain situations only; this has made us realise that there is not one simple thing called 'advertising', but a large collection of different types of advertising which work in different ways for different objectives.

Another reason for progress is that more and more circumstantial evidence has been published, notably in the *Advertising*

Works series of case histories[50-55] which have won the IPA Advertising Effectiveness Awards, and also elsewhere, in which it has been possible to infer convincingly that an effect must have been due to the advertising, because nothing else can explain it. These cases tend to be ones where clear objectives have been set for the advertising (surely no coincidence), so that one can draw conclusions which add to understanding as well as demonstrating success. It is also true that we have in many respects more and better quality data available to study, although it may be argued that we do not yet invest enough in studying it. All in all, compared with even twenty years ago, we understand more about the complexity of what we are dealing with; at the same time, we have been comforted by being able to prove to ourselves the possibility that, when the circumstances are right, advertising does work, because we can see and measure it.

However, as has often been said, the published cases are a small percentage of the total. We do not hear of the many more cases where the advertising does not work as intended, or, more likely, where it is not clear whether or how it has done so. To the extent that this knowledge is lacking, those who set budgets and design marketing plans must depend on a more subjective vision, perhaps coloured by personal prejudice or company culture. It is still agreed that there is much waste in advertising[59]. Our position is better than it was, but it is far from good enough.

What exactly are we talking about?
One of the major problems in discussing this subject is the difficulty of agreeing the terms. Each word in the phrase 'how advertising works' could be preceded by the well known debating catchphrase: 'it depends what you mean by …'. For example, 'advertising': at what level (its macro effect on the economy, at the level of a product category, of a brand?) – in what form (a single advertisement at a point in time, a burst, a

continuous sequence, a whole campaign lasting years?) – in relation to whom (an exposed consumer, several exposed consumers, people with opportunities to see, a group, a whole population?) – over what time span (an hour, a day, a week, a month, a year, a purchase cycle period?). Again, 'works' – do we mean effects on sales (if so, what sales? ex-factory, retailer level, consumer level?) or on consumers' minds? If the latter, is it perception, absorption of information, emotional response, or what? Are we talking about psychology or statistics? Failure to agree, or to realise that one disagrees, about the terms of the discussion can easily lead to a dialogue of the deaf. It is made harder by the fact that some of the terminology frequently used, for example long- and short-term effects or 'brand equity', are not simple concepts to grasp and may mean different things to different people.

There is also a constant need to beware of the research naming fallacy (I am indebted for this to Stephen King). It goes like this:

All advertising must work by 'persuasion' (or something else).

I have a research method called a 'persuasion measure'.

Therefore it measures advertising effectiveness.

The term 'persuasion' can slide from one meaning to the other during an argument without being noticed. Another dangerous word is 'attitude', which can be used both to refer to the totality of a person's relationship with a brand and whatever is being measured in a tracking study by an 'attitude battery'. The measure is always an artefact constructed to represent, as well as we can, a reality we can never quite know in full, and it is only one of a number of possible artefacts which could have been constructed.

At various points in the review we shall come back to this need to define precisely what we mean before we can understand an argument.

Plan of this review

In this review, we look at advertising effectiveness at different levels of discourse:

1. *At the macro level: markets and economies* – effects on economies, on markets and on brands within markets.

2. *Sales effectiveness of advertising* – how this can be understood, observed and interpreted.

3. *How people respond to advertising: effects on the mind* – how we conceptualise people's response to, or use of, advertising.

4. *What kinds of response are possible?* – ways of thinking about the desired response to specific advertising, and predicting and assessing its achievement.

All of these are aspects of the overall question: what are the features (rules, constraints) which define advertising and indicate its strengths and limitations? They follow a logical order, going from the 'macro' to the 'micro', from advertising in general down to how individual advertisements can be perceived by their targets, like a series of nesting boxes.

The literature, and acknowledgements

In preparing this review, I have read and revisited what I believe to have been the most significant contributions to the subject during the past twenty to thirty years. I am conscious that it is still only a small proportion of the total literature: our continued ignorance about advertising is certainly not a function of the number of words written about it. I have attempted to be selective, concentrating on those authors who have genuinely taken our understanding forward, and to be as up-to-date as possible.

I am extremely grateful to a number of people who have helped me in the literature search and who have been kind enough to read and comment on my manuscript in its first draft: they include Mike Waterson and the library of the Advertising Association under Philip Spink, Simon Broadbent, John Philip Jones, Stephen King, Winston Fletcher, and Mike Naples and staff at the Advertising Research Foundation, New York. Their advice has been very valuable indeed. Errors, opinions and interpretations are all down to me, unless otherwise stated.

2 Summary

Advertising is so varied that almost anything we ever say about it is liable to be refuted by some contrary example. Yet we recognise advertising when we see it. For example, a commercial for a soap powder, a press or poster ad for a new car, and a circular from a bank describing a loan scheme are all very different, but we have no difficulty in seeing them all as 'advertising', and having something in common that they do *not* share with, for example, a banded offer or a price cut on the same soap powder, or free insurance offered with the same car. And we would readily agree that the distinctiveness we recognise as 'advertising' has something to do with the way it works – even if in the next breath we go on to say that we don't know how it does.

The purpose of this book is to draw together what we know about 'advertising' (which may be more than we think), and to try to clarify the confusions that surround the question of what it is and how it works. This has a direct practical value. There are two kinds of traps which people can and do fall into, if the essential nature of advertising is not grasped. One is over-confidence: to expect something of advertising which it is not fitted to achieve, and be disappointed when it inevitably fails. The other is impatience: failing to recognise what advertising can do uniquely, abandoning it too soon, and risking the loss of one's market in the process. Marketing practice has always been, and is still (perhaps more than ever), in danger from both these errors. Time spent trying to get our minds clear about advertising in general, even though it may seem rather abstract, will not be wasted if these traps can be more easily avoided.

The questions raised and discussed are summarised below.

1. At the macro level: markets and economies
(i) Does advertising expand markets, or does it only work to

position brands within a market? We discuss the limited evidence available, which seems to point to the latter conclusion in most cases.

(ii) We discuss the concept of, and the evidence for, markets being in *equilibrium*, having reached the limit of potential growth. In developed economies, markets are increasingly in this state or tending towards it. We look at the place of advertising in bringing about and maintaining the 'dynamic equilibrium' between competitive, differentiated brands.

(iii) The relation of advertising to price is covered: both in justifying a premium through branding and in keeping market prices down through competition. Advertising can be seen as a lubricant of the competitive process. The benefits of gaining leadership in a market, and the contrasting difficulty of breaking into a new market successfully, are part of this question.

2. Sales effectiveness of advertising

(i) Advertising has a 'long-term' as well as a 'short-term' effect (unlike most promotions, which are necessarily transitory). This 'dual personality' has been the source of much confusion. We propose a more productive way of thinking about sales effects, avoiding this troublesome dichotomy.

(ii) We discuss the two available ways of measuring sales effects: econometrics and (in the USA but not yet widely elsewhere) single-source panel data. Both face the same problem: they only work well if sales show short-term incremental movements. In many cases with established brands, sales effects fail to show; yet there is reason to believe that the advertising is doing a good job for the brand, maintaining its long-term position, and that to

18

abandon it (eg in favour of promotions that spend revenue for a temporary gain) may be very dangerous.

(iii) The task of distinguishing between advertising which is successfully supporting a brand, even though we cannot 'see' it in sales increments, and advertising which is ineffective and should be changed, is perhaps the most important problem awaiting solution in advertising effectiveness measurement. It is suggested that the solution cannot be found through aggregate sales measures, but only by looking at the level of individuals and identifying those who actually respond. This could be done by a different approach to single-source panel data, which takes the analysis down to individuals. Techniques for doing this have been proposed in the past, but the approach has yet to be adopted, including by those US services such as IRI who are purveying single-source data.

(iv) Sales analysis at the individual level is also the best way to sort out confusions and interactions between advertising and other influences (price, distribution, couponing, etc).

3. How people respond to advertising: effects on the mind

(i) We need more than sales results to tell us how and why people respond to advertising, including those cases where immediate purchasing is not the appropriate or expected response. How does advertising affect the mental perception, and can this help us to distinguish between what works and what does not?

(ii) How people respond to advertisements can obviously be very complex, but there is evidence that many people, including practitioners in the advertising process, tend to adopt a simplified, intuitive, common-sense 'model' of the response advertising is intended to evoke. Such simple models ('persuasion', 'involvement' and so on) seem to be part of the culture. The danger could be that they may be preconceptions which obscure what really happens in the mind of the target audience when confronted with a particular advertisement.

(iii) Underlying these perceptions are two basic, opposite mental orientations: one, that consumers are essentially *passive* and moved by advertising, the other that consumers are essentially *active*, making choices and selecting which advertising they will attend to or not. It is argued that these are alternative intuitive ways of interpreting the world, which cannot be proved or disproved, but are very important in shaping and developing the views individuals hold of how advertising works. In recent years, there has been a substantial cultural shift away from the 'passive' towards the 'active' consumer view; this is exemplified in the abandonment of sequential models (DAGMAR, etc) and the recognition of the importance of selective perception, accurate target setting and the emotional elements in consumer response. It is noted that the old sequential models can still be appropriate in some cases, and that the underlying 'passive consumer' ideology is by no means universally dead.

(iv) Another hypothesis discussed is that advertising, rather than producing an instant reaction, works by implanting a relevant association in the long-term memory, to be retrieved at the appropriate time (eg at the point of sale). This complements the concept of the long-term sales effect of advertising.

4. What kinds of response are possible?

(i) Every advertisement is a unique creative activity. But successful practitioners have codified ways of thinking about the task, or 'rules of thumb', which they have found helpful and wish to pass on. Two examples are given for illustration: one, a scheme for thinking out the primary role of the campaign; the other, for placing the brand in terms of the two crucial dimensions of degree of involvement (with the product) and how rational or emotional the decision is for the consumer.

(ii) The importance of 'liking' (in its widest sense, including 'finding relevant and meaningful') is discussed. Recent research from America (the ARF's Copy Research Validity Project) has reinforced the importance of 'liking', as well as traditional measures of recall and persuasion, as a predictor of advertising success. This leads to a consideration of the value of copy-testing: not as a predictor of what *will* happen, but a reassurance that the advertisement is likely to achieve its objectives coupled with diagnosis of where and how it can be improved. The shift to interest in diagnosis as more useful than prediction of sales is part of the cultural shift noted earlier towards the notion of the 'active' consumer.

(iii) Advertisers need to know what is wrong with an advertisement and how to put it right. Our diagnostic methods are not yet very good at supplying this need. It is suggested that the next task for the future should be to develop a background of theory about how advertisements communicate, so that we could get away from relying on norms and anecdotes when we are trying to assess whether a particular advertisement is communicating (or affecting consumers) as we wish. Academic disciplines such as communication theory should be more in evidence in this field.

(iv) There is also a discussion of saturation (ie an advertisement ceasing to have an 'effect', because we are bored with it): the importance of defining one's terms (what 'effect' are we talking about?) and the timing (how long a gap is needed for the message to become refreshed).

From these questions, certain threads can be drawn together; we can set out under broad headings a number of 'rules of the game'. These are proposed in the final section, along with some implications. Understanding these 'rules' does not limit creative freedom, but rather enhances its effect, because it helps us to ensure that we use advertising in line with its strengths and avoid its points of weakness. It will help also to dispel the misunderstandings which surround advertising among its political enemies, as well as those users who may be feeling disillusioned.

3 At the macro level: markets and economies

Can advertising increase a whole market? It is unusual to start at this level of question; most discussions, if they mention it at all, consign it to an inconclusive paragraph at the end. It is the hardest level at which to show even the faintest evidence of advertising making things happen.

However, it is important to start here, for two reasons. One is that this is the level at which politicians argue, and are able to build up false images of advertising (whether as a force for good or evil does not matter) which are based on little more substantial than their own prejudices. We need to take a view on how far we can follow them. The other reason is that unless we have some understanding of the economic context within which advertising operates, it is impossible to see it in perspective.

Two types of argument
There are, essentially, two kinds of opposing argument, as follows:

1. Advertising increases, or at least helps to increase, the total demand for a product. That means that it does actually bring it about, somehow, that significant numbers of people do something which they would not have done without it, eg become customers or increase their custom; advertising can alter their will and change their habits. It is therefore logical to curb advertising which supports a socially undesirable habit, such as smoking or alcohol, and to support advertising which will change people's attitudes in a benign direction, as in the context of AIDS or not driving after drinking.

2. Advertising does not affect people's basic orientations and drives, but rather the choices they make when seeking to

23

fulfil them. No advertising ever made someone buy a product when he did not want to, or buy more of it than he needed, or change his beliefs about what he ought to do. Advertising works with the grain of people's desires, never against it. It is about choosing brands, and only that, in the context of behaviour already decided. It is therefore illogical to seek to reduce an undesirable habit or promote a desirable attitude by controlling advertising; it will have no effect at that level. Most government advertising is a waste of money.

These arguments are deliberately stated in an extreme form: few opponents of advertising controls would wish to go as far as the last sentence, for example. There are very plausible elements in both. Even if we generally accept the position that advertising does not lead people to act against their will, should we not worry about the weak-willed and vulnerable? If they are on the edge already, it can be hard not to believe that advertising may be just the thing to tip them over. There is a competition in ideas as well as products; if we see offensive and harmful ideas being publicised, should we not counteract them?

Evidence about markets
Advertising does not affect competitive market size
Such evidence as there is seems to suggest that at the macro level of a market, as opposed to the individual brand, advertising does not affect overall growth or decline in demand. Jones[40,57] quotes an exception: in the fifteen years from 1960, the Californian Avocado Advisory Board embarked on an advertising and publicity campaign to increase the primary demand for avocados; its success was demonstrated by the fact that the average returns per acre more than tripled during the period, a far higher increase than the rate of inflation (in an agricultural market like this, price closely follows demand and is an accurate measure of increase in demand; since the adver-

tising was the only variable to have changed, it was clearly responsible for the increase).

In this case, advertising plainly increased total demand in a product field. But the key factor was that there was no counter-vailing competition; there is only one avocado. In most categories of consumer goods, as Jones puts it: 'much of the advertising's successful stimulation of the demand for one specific brand is going to be countered by the advertising and promotion of competitive brands.' When the context for adver-tising is *competitive*, as is usually the case, the advertising and promotion for different brands tend to cancel out. Consumers move towards a brand in response to advertising, perhaps, but in so doing they move away from other brands; they do not increase their total use.

It is necessary to be a little careful in distinguishing 'brands' and 'markets'; in reality, there are often several levels of aggregation. Harp is a brand of lager, but lager is only one kind of beer. Perhaps advertising for lager brands may, all together, stimulate growth in lager as a whole at the expense of other beers. Even in the avocado case, the increased sales of avocado might have been offset by reductions for other vegetables or salads. Waterson[107] has proposed that we should think in terms of a hierarchy of 'levels of market', as follows:

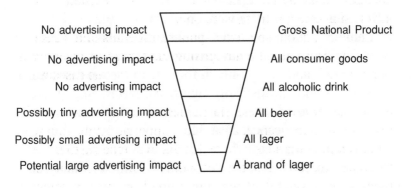

No advertising impact	Gross National Product
No advertising impact	All consumer goods
No advertising impact	All alcoholic drink
Possibly tiny advertising impact	All beer
Possibly small advertising impact	All lager
Potential large advertising impact	A brand of lager

However, keeping that qualification in mind, we will stay with 'brands' and 'markets' to simplify the argument. Most of the limited evidence supports the view that, in competitive markets, advertising does not seem to have an effect in making the market as a whole grow, unless it was set to grow anyway. Henry[46] analysed eighteen food product categories, comparing sales against advertising weights, both at constant prices, for the years 1975 to 1983. Manufacturers' sales were taken from *The Food and Drink Forecast*, advertising expenditures from MEAL, corrected by the Advertising Association formula which adjusts for rate card variations. In all eighteen cases, no consistent relationships were found. Henry concluded that: 'To the question which forms the title of this paper – does advertising affect total market size? – my answer must be, at least in respect of the product categories which I have here discussed, that it does not appear to do so in any general way or to any material extent.' He goes on: 'It could be argued, of course, that these product categories are mature markets, and cannot be expected to show much change, with or without advertising. If that were true it would beg the main question, but in fact it is not true. As we have seen, even in these mature markets there are considerable variations from year to year, together with longer-term changes in both directions – such variations and changes being quite sufficient to reveal the existence of an advertising effect if there were one.'

Lambin[74], quoted by Jones, published details of ten cases in which he estimated the advertising elasticity* of category as opposed to brand sales. Only in four out of the ten cases was it possible to find a statistically significant advertising elasticity at the market level. These elasticities were small and at a very low level of significance, 25%. More importantly, the four were all developing markets, where demand was tending to increase for other reasons. Another economist, Simon[97], analysed a range of empirical data and found no clear 'macro' effect of advertising on markets as a whole.

Mature markets have nowhere to grow

The same conclusion has been argued by other authors over the years (eg Borden[13], writing in 1942). It is supported by the general observation that *many, if not most, consumer markets are mature*, and do not show the overall growth which one would expect if the volume of advertising applied to them was effective in making whole markets grow.

By a 'mature market' we mean one in which the capacity of the population to buy the product or take up the service has been fully used up: there will be no additional new buyers except in so far as increases in the population will provide them, and all those who buy are doing so as much and as often as they want. There is little or no scope for advertising or any other persuasive influence to increase either the number of buyers or the frequency with which they buy, in total: if a brand increases it can only be at other brands' expense.

Fast-moving consumer goods markets (FMCG for short) are particularly likely to be 'mature' in this sense, at least in the developed economies. We have to beware, here and throughout, of the 'FMCG fallacy', which slips into thinking that, because most evidence and therefore literature about advertising

Advertising elasticity. It is important to understand the meaning of this term. Advertising elasticity is defined as the percentage change in offtake following a 1% change in advertising spend (Roberts[95]; Broadbent[17]; Jones[60,61]). Broadbent[17] published for 84 brands an average elasticity of 0.2: this means that a 1% increase in advertising produced, on average, a 0.2% increase in sales. An increase of 10% in advertising would, by the same token, produce an average 2% increase in sales. 30 out of the 84 brands had elasticities of 0.2 or over; on the other hand, 27 of them had elasticities between 0 and 0.09, much less likely to be profitable.

The *breakeven* level of elasticity is that at which the increased revenue from the extra sales is equal to the cost of the extra advertising: above that point, the advertising is profitable, below it the return is negative.

This definition still leaves open how one defines the terms used: eg, what is meant by 'short-term' or 'advertising spend'.

happens to be based on FMCGs, therefore all advertising is like that. Jones[58] quotes from a review carried out by J Walter Thompson worldwide, which yielded information about 1,096 brands in 23 countries: 79% of these brands were repeat-purchase packaged goods and 21% were other types of goods and services. He reports the following relationship:

	Packaged goods	Non-packaged goods
Markets that are:		
Growing strongly	32%	(73%)
Growing weakly	23%	(9%)
Flat	30%	(4%)
Declining	15%	(14%)

Brackets in the second column indicate a small sample base of only 45 markets, as opposed to 170 markets in the packaged goods group.

Jones qualifies the figures in this table by pointing out that they are unweighted by market size, and that it is the larger and longer-established markets which tend to be flat or declining. The 68% of packaged goods markets that are in the lowest categories of growth should therefore receive a heavier emphasis than what is shown in the table. 'This means that, in general, much the largest majority of *substantial* and *established* markets for packaged goods show little total growth. The situation with other types of goods and services is different, although the strong increase in many of these markets is also accompanied by considerable volatility. It is nevertheless important for clients and agencies to look outside the packaged goods field for the most substantial future sales increases. And agencies in particular – as they have recently discovered to their cost – can expect only sluggish growth in the advertising budgets of their traditional packaged goods clients.'

That a majority of FMCG markets are 'mature' in the sense explained above should not be taken to imply that economies have necessarily stopped growing. There has been shifting to other services; new ways are constantly being invented to enable people to spend their money. The concept of maturity ties back to the individual level: there is simply a limit to the amount an individual or household will ever *want* to consume, for a number of familiar products, and when that limit has been reached the market is 'mature'.

The trend towards 'maturity' is particularly a feature of developed economies. In a later paper[60], Jones speaks of how consumer goods markets in the United States have been 'inexorably maturing – and gradually stagnating.' They have been slowing in aggregate growth and eventually, in one market after another, 'stabilizing in total volume, except for annual increases of 1% or 2% caused mainly by population growth.' During the 1970s the number of stabilized markets overtook the number of still growing markets: data from Mediamark Research showed that only 13 out of 150 large consumer goods markets grew by more than 10% in 1989. This lack of market vitality 'appears irreversible, since it represents a seemingly permanent ceiling on consumers' purchase levels in all except a few areas – mainly financial and other services and high-tech, not the traditional categories of packaged goods and consumer durables. A number of important markets, including cigarettes, coffee, dairy products and hard liquor, are actually declining.' Jones argues that this trend towards stabilization has had a major effect on manufacturers' perceptions of their marketing goals, especially the key importance of market share; this in turn has fuelled the reliance on promotions to deliver immediate sales increases, the cutting of longer-term investment in theme advertising and R&D in order to prune costs, and the tendency to give away profit in promotions in order to maintain market share. 'Competition has become increasingly aggressive as manufacturers react in frustration to what they see as the inertia of markets. Their yardstick of success is market share. The initial competitive drive and the reaction it generates can cancel one another out ... But producers' concentration on sales volume has caused them to neglect the price they pay and the earnings they are obliged to sacrifice as a result of the marketing plans they embark on so optimistically[60].'

Developed markets have their own momentum

If high levels of advertising fail to increase a mature market, reduced levels seem to have little effect on markets which consumers wish to support. Cigarette advertising was removed from television in early 1971, and for several years after, in the USA, and in the following decade there was massive unfavourable publicity about the effects of smoking on health. In spite of this, cigarette consumption did not begin to decline until 1981, ten years later[57].

In Quebec, in 1991, a case was brought by certain tobacco manufacturers against the ban on tobacco advertising which had been operative in Canada during the previous three years. In the judgement, the advertising ban was overturned on the ground that it violated the constitutional right to free speech. One of the papers submitted on the side of the defence (in favour of the ban) came from the Health Protection Branch (Tobacco Products Unit). In this paper, which was of course hostile to cigarette advertising, the following admission was made:

'Department officials have examined virtually all the econometric and sociological studies that examine the relationship between advertising and consumption. They have also examined the experiences of all countries that have banned tobacco advertising. However, no clear picture emerges from quantitative analysis of this relationship. From these data, no conclusive case can be advanced to either support or refute the argument that banning tobacco advertising will, in and of itself, reduce tobacco consumption in Canada.'[28]

The importance of competition

From such evidence as this, the conclusion we draw is not that advertising can never affect a market as a whole, but that most of the time it does not. Advertising is not strong enough to be the main driving force in market or social change; but if other forces are driving a change, advertising will help to shape the way it comes about. If the conditions are right for a new market to form (the Sony Walkman, for example), advertising will contribute to its growth, and will influence the emerging distribution of brands. If people are socially ready for a change of attitude, for example, that it is no longer respectable to drink if one is driving, advertising will work with the social pressure; without that pressure, it may well be helpless. It may even help to create the pressure, but against the competition of other influences and entrenched habits it is likely to take a very long time.

In both marketing and social contexts, advertising is inhibited by competition. It can only work with the grain of people's wishes, not against them. In competitive markets, unless there is a reason for demand to change, established needs and habits provide the framework within which brands struggle for share, and the playing field for advertising is set. In social marketing, there is a competitive market of ideas, established for other reasons and even harder to shift unless there is, independently, a driving force for change.

Effects at brand/company level within markets

The evidence so far has been light and circumstantial, but it seems to point only one way: advertising does not seem to affect the total size of markets except in the rare cases where there is no competition.

What are the forces that shape markets?

In theory

Jones[57,61] has pulled together a wide range of evidence and given a succinct account of this very complex subject, which carries much conviction not least because it is both up to date and lucid. His explanation is as follows.

1. *Oligopolistic competition.* Most developed consumer markets are *oligopolies.* That means that all the demand in the market is satisfied by a relatively small number of suppliers who compete intensely with each other. Each company has obtained a share of the market, and the way this is done is by *differentiating* their product so that it builds up its own franchise of loyal consumers who like the *particular* values exemplified in this product compared to the others. This process of product differentiation is known as *branding.*

2. *Economies of scale.* The different company brands in the market occupy different shares, some much larger than others. When a company has obtained a relatively large share for its brand, it benefits from a number of economies of scale, which assist it to maintain that share. Production, marketing and distribution costs, including advertising, tend to be lower as a proportion of sales (though not lower in absolute terms) for larger brands. Also, a company which already has a well-established brand name in the field can more easily extend its product range. New entrants to the market are deterred, since they have to pay a much higher premium in marketing costs, and this keeps the number of competitors in the market limited.

3. *Brand-based premium corrected by price competition.* Branding, by adding value, enables a premium price to be charged; customers are generally willing to pay more for a brand that is distinctively different in a way they like. But, beyond a certain point, the brand becomes vulnerable to lower price competition. In this way, prices across the market as a whole are stabilised, whilst variations in pricing are one of the principal ways in which rival brands seek competitive advantage. In an oligopoly, there is price elasticity, which means that as a manufacturer increases his price he will lose sales. It is in his interest to reduce this elasticity for his own brand; the more he can make it distinctive by branding, the higher the price he will be able to charge. Brands, in most markets, command a higher price than generics or own labels which have the same functional characteristics, and this is a function of the willingness of consumers to pay a premium for differentiation.

4. *Tendency to equilibrium.* A market described in this way tends towards *equilibrium*. In other words, when the market is mature, the companies in it have acquired varying shares by the process of differentiating their products into brands and, in so doing, satisfying the different needs consumers may have. Competition, in price and alternative branding, limits the power of each player to increase share or reduce price elasticity. At the same time, new entrants to the market are deterred by the high cost of entry against established positions with their attached economies of scale. This equilibrium is not uniform: companies are constantly battling to gain advantage against each other by various promotional methods including pricing; the market may be disturbed by the entry of something new, based on a different formulation, new technology, something to satisfy a previously unnoticed gap; sometimes these incursions may change the total picture

permanently, and there may be a period of discordance until it settles down again into a new pattern. Inter-company competition is likely to be intense and aggressive. But, on the surface, the competing pressures cancel out. Equilibrium, except in a new and growing market, is the norm to which things tend.

A study by a leading American marketing consultant, James C. Schroer, of a number of stable developed markets showed that they tend to be dominated by two or three major brands, which are easily able to maintain their positions against attack because they can afford to pour in enough advertising dollars to ensure that the equilibrium in the market is always restored. No smaller competitor, however aggressive, can afford to continue spending at the level needed to permanently jack up its share. Typically, the leader will have a larger advertising Share of Voice than its competitor, but smaller in relation to its Share of Market. If the competitor were able to sustain a substantially higher spend, raising its Share of Voice 20-30% above the leader, it could well alter the equilibrium in its favour. Schroer found that this often happens in the United States in individual geographical markets, because advertising budgets are set on a national basis ignoring market differences.[96]

Empirical confirmation: the Ehrenberg models

This summary picture of mature competitive markets appears highly consistent with all the factual evidence we have. The most important such evidence comes in the work of Andrew Ehrenberg and his colleagues at the London Business School. Over the years they have built up an empirically based account of the way that frequently bought packaged goods markets work. The data they have used are taken from purchase records for the same samples of households over long periods of time; they cover more than fifty product fields, both food and nonfood, different pack sizes, several different countries including the USA and Europe, a thirty-year-plus time span, various demographic sub-groups, time-periods ranging from a week to twelve months, and different techniques of consumer panel measurement. What is important is that, over this huge range of products, covering widely different market sizes and brand-switching frequencies and patterns, the same lawlike regularities occur: so much so that one can safely predict the patterns of purchasing behaviour for any brand in any category, once one knows its market share. This is tantamount to saying that we know the *mechanism* by which all the brands in a market reach and maintain their state of equilibrium (Ehrenberg[29, 30]).

When markets are stationary (in equilibrium), which was the case with nearly all the markets studied, Ehrenberg found patterns of consumer behaviour which were highly consistent. From these, he developed models which accurately predicted actual observed behaviour. The models have been validated on so wide a scale now that the generalisations they enshrine must be taken as standard; no theory, of advertising or anything else, applied to stable packaged goods markets, which conflicts with the Ehrenberg models can be accepted without severe scrutiny.

The key elements of the pattern Ehrenberg and his colleagues have found in stationary markets can be summarised as follows:

1. Brands vary considerably in *penetration*, that is, the proportion of buyers of the field who buy them. In any two periods of equal length, the penetration of any brand is similar: about the same proportion of product buyers buy that brand in both periods.

2. For any brand, some buyers buy it much more infrequently than others. In a short period, there will be relatively few buyers; as periods increase in length (eg, to a month or a

quarter instead of a week), the penetration will increase, because there are more infrequent purchasers buying in the longer period.

3. The average purchase frequency for any brand tends to be low: for example, in a 13-week period in the breakfast cereal market, the average number of purchases per buyer varied only between 1.8 and 2.7. The penetrations of these brands varied much more. This means that the frequency distribution for any brand is highly skewed: whatever its share, it has many more infrequent than frequent purchasers, and the distributions are similar between brands of different shares. There is one exception to this: the average purchase frequency tends to be somewhat higher when a brand has reached a high absolute level of penetration. This appears to be an economy of scale effect. Average purchase frequencies remain virtually constant for any brand between periods of equal length, whether they follow each other or not.

4. The models can predict the repeat purchase rate, ie the proportion of purchasers in one period who will buy the same brand in another period. These proportions increase for longer periods, and are similar between brands, but again there is an economy of scale effect, in that brands with large penetrations tend to have larger than average repurchase rates.

5. Few buyers of any brand buy only that brand. Solus buyers buy the brand at the same frequency as do the much larger number who buy more than one brand. Multibrand buying also shows a remarkable consistency: the *duplication of purchase law*. It is found that the buyer of any one brand will also buy any second brand in direct proportion to the penetration of the second brand. This means that if Brand X is

bought by 11% of buyers of Brand A, it will also be bought by 11% of buyers of Brands B, C, D etc. These proportions are not exactly the same as the penetration of Brand X, but a constant multiple of it, usually a little more than one; this multiple, the 'duplication coefficient', tends to be higher between brands which are competing closely with each other for the same set of consumer needs.

The picture provided by the Ehrenberg models is consistent with that of the market in equilibrium between differentiated brands of different shares, and strengthens it by the insight given into consumer habits. Consumer behaviour in the aggregate exhibits certain regularities, which contribute to stability and the limitation of demand, even though individual consumers may vary very greatly in the different buying patterns they show in panel records. Buyers have families of needs which are satisfied by different brands; they like variety. It is rare for one brand to appeal exclusively to one distinct group of consumers. Brands grow, not by increasing the proportion of heavy users, but by increasing the total number of users, their usage frequency distribution remaining the same.

It is important to understand that the last sentence is not meant to be prescriptive. We are saying that, when a brand grows in a stable market, *what happens* is that the proportion of product buyers who buy the brand grows but that their average frequency (and therefore the proportion of heavy to light buyers, etc) does not. We are *not* saying that this is how to achieve the result. The Ehrenberg findings have often seemed paradoxical and difficult to accept because they seem to suggest, for example, that one cannot promote a brand by persuading users that they should use it more often or in a different way, since only the penetration of the brand can grow, not the frequency of use. But it is quite possible that persuading users to become heavier users might be a very good way of building up a brand; in the same advertising process, new light users would be sucked in at the bottom end, and we would still end up with the Ehrenberg result of a brand with more buyers but the same average frequency (concealing, in most cases, a very wide distribution of different frequencies). Ehrenberg does not tell us how to change a brand's position in a market; what he tells us is how that market will settle down again after the change has occurred, before the next upheaval.

An important practical implication of these models is the power it can give us to predict sales targets accurately. Once we know the penetration of a brand, we can immediately predict other things about it, such as the frequencies with which its buyers will buy it in a period, will buy other brands, etc. This can be used to set the penetration target for a new brand: by predicting the sales deliverable at different penetration levels, one can see at what level the brand must settle down if it is to deliver a profitable level of sales, and can determine the promotion needed to achieve that. We can be confident about this. 'A major exception, such as that the new brand might turn out to have a repeat-rate as high as six, ie twice the predicted value of about three, would be revolutionary. It could only occur if the new brand were to differ more radically from any of the existing brands than *any of these differ from each other.*' (Ehrenberg[29])

Other things we know support this picture of the equilibrial market. Most new brand launches fail; it is difficult and costly to gain a foothold against established brands, with their scale economies, unless one has a very good story to tell. Estimates taken from various surveys of the percentage of new brands which fail have ranged from 40% to 95%; only two of these were under 50%, and four were over 70% (Jones[61]). It has further been pointed out to me that many of the surveys, particularly in America, do not distinguish well between new brands and new products, and that many of the 'successes' are in fact brand or line extensions. The failure rate for new brands, strictly defined, is thus likely to be 90% or more. A new brand introduction can disturb the market for a short time, but it settles down quickly, even if a small amount of room has been made for the new brand.

The PIMS database

Further evidence for the value of a strong brand position comes from the work of The Strategic Planning Institute[9, 88]. This body manages a unique database known as PIMS (standing for 'profit impact of market strategy'). The PIMS database contains detailed information on more than 2,700 businesses for a minimum of four years each; it is the only database in the world that includes both marketing and financial information. A joint research project by the SPI and what was then the Ogilvy Center for Research and Development (later part of the WPP group, and now sadly defunct), reporting in 1987[88], showed that market share and 'perceived quality' both relate positively to profitability as measured by return on investment (ROI). 'Perceived quality' in this project was derived from product test results, and thus relates to part of what we mean by 'branding' (ie physical or functional differences observed between products, but not the psychological values which may attach to undifferentiated products). Consumer companies with market shares above 40% obtain ROIs of 41% on average; at the other end of the scale, companies with market shares below 10% earn ROIs averaging about 9%. Similarly, when consumers think the 'perceived quality' is superior, ROI averages 31%; when quality is thought to be inferior, average ROI drops to 17% (see Figure 1). Cross-linking the two variables, companies with large market shares and superior perceived quality earn dramatically larger ROIs than those at the opposite end of the scale, as the table shows:

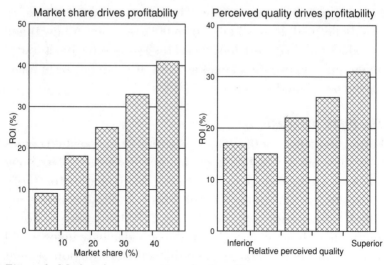

Figure 1. Market share versus perceived quality

	Market share		
	Small	Medium	Large
'Quality'			
Inferior	11%	18%	29%
Medium	9%	20%	29%
Superior	16%	27%	43%

The SPI comment in their report as follows:

'Economic theory and intuition tell us businesses that offer superior perceived quality achieve several key benefits:

- stronger customer loyalty
- more repeat purchases
- less vulnerability to price wars.

The PIMS Competitive Strategy Data Base indicates that key benefits of superior perceived quality also include:

- lower marketing costs
- ability to command higher relative price without affecting share
- share improvements at comparable prices.

They also comment:

'A strong competitive position can increase profitability in several ways: first, large-share businesses enjoy scale economies in working capital, marketing, research and development, and other cost components. Second, they enjoy economies of cumulative volume, which reduce unit costs (the experience-curve effect) and spread set-up costs over a longer production run. Third, to avoid making a poor choice of vendor, buyers often favour large-share businesses, giving dominant suppliers an advantage. Finally, large-share businesses often have greater bargaining power with both customers and suppliers and are frequently able to take the initiative against their competitors.'

How advertising helps to shape markets

Advertising helps to bring about and to keep in being the equilibrial situation we have been describing. It does this in two main ways. First, it is a major force in establishing the product differentiation which achieves branding and market share. Secondly, it fuels the competition which leads to 'dynamic equilibrium'.

Jones[57] traces a sequence of theoretical stages in which

advertising operates.

1. *In the short term, advertising tends towards increasing demand, which can then tend to raise the effective price.* It is very difficult to observe this in real life, because to do so one has to 'freeze' the initial advertising effect before competitive counter-measures are felt. The avocado case mentioned previously is quoted, and another anonymous example in which 'the demand curve was shifted to the right': that is, it can be shown that in the second period of measurement, a given level of output commanded 'a strikingly higher price' than in the earlier period. Because the advertising campaign was the only important change in the marketing mix between the two periods, one could reliably say that the price rise was due to the advertising. Another example which could be quoted is the Kellogg's Rice Krispies case reported in the first edition of *Advertising Works*, a collection of papers from the IPA Advertising Effectiveness Awards[33,50]. This showed a new campaign moving the 'demand curve' decisively to the right. The 'demand curve' is the inverse relationship familiar to economists between quantity purchased and price: as the price rises, the quantity falls (quantity being shown on the vertical axis of the graph, price on the horizontal axis). If the demand curve moves to the right, it means that a price increase will still deliver the same quantity purchased, and the same price will deliver a larger volume, whilst the relationship between price and quantity remains the same. Figure 2 will make this clear. The observed shift signified 'a rise in the perceived *value* of Rice Krispies accompanied by a rise in the proportion of month-by-month sales variation that was due to price'.

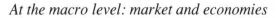

Figure 2. The shift in the demand curve for Rice Krispies

2. *Advertising lubricates competition*. Price increases are seldom allowed to get out of hand, because competitors quickly respond. Where there is price elasticity, too high a price will lose sales, and therefore share, to the competition.

One of the ways in which advertising helps to keep prices lower through competitive action is that it is an effective means of spreading information about competitive prices. A classic study by Benham[5] compared prices for eyeglasses between American states which allowed opticians to advertise and those which banned advertising; he found that prices for comparable products averaged $33 when advertising was banned, but only $26 where it was allowed; the mean price in the most restrictive state was more than twice that in the least restrictive state. This study was later followed by two studies sponsored by the Federal Trade Commission into the costs of eye examinations and eyeglasses and the cost of cosmetic contact lens fitting services. In the FTC report[34] it is stated that:

43

'These studies provide important evidence that state restrictions which prevent or hinder the development of optometric chain firms and other commercial optometrists raise prices to consumers. The BE study found that prices were significantly lower in markets with chain firms; all types of providers... charged lower prices in markets with chain firms and prices were lower at all levels of quality... The Contact Lens Study corroborates these findings. It found that commercial firms charged less than non-commercial firms, suggesting that restrictions on such firms, by limiting competition, are likely to raise prices throughout the market and deny consumers access to a low-cost alternative.' (Bureau of Consumer Protection, 1986)

The same report also quoted evidence that the absence of restrictions on commercial practice, including advertising, did not prejudice quality.

A similar effect was found from ending the ban on advertising of legal services in the USA: a study by Cox found that: 'the level of fees attorneys charge for each of four routine legal services... was found to vary inversely with the relative restrictiveness of a state's regulations on attorney advertising practices.' (Waterson[107]; Jones[57]).

The scale economies obtained by brands with large and established market shares define the scope for competition and the role of advertising in promoting it. Larger brands can afford to outspend smaller ones, as demonstrated in the PIMS study (Biel[9]): they have larger advertising to sales ratios, as the following composite table makes clear:

	Average market share %	Average perceived quality %	Average ROI %
A:S ratios v. direct competitors			
Much less	14	44	17
Less	20	50	22
Equal	25	56	22
More	26	60	25
Much more	32	69	32

At the same time, the relative costs of achieving their sales, including advertising, are much lower than for smaller brands. Jones has developed a chart, which has become known as a Jones diagram (Broadbent[18]), which compares a brand's Share of Voice (its share of the total advertising in the market) to its Share of the Market (Figure 3). Where a brand's Share of Voice (SOV) is larger than its Share of Market (SOM), it is investing at a higher than average rate. From a study of 666 different packaged goods, Jones has shown that brands with relatively low market shares must invest comparatively much more in advertising than brands with large shares.

This sets the terms for new brands seeking to enter a market and for small brands seeking to grow. And it enshrines the place of advertising; unless they pay a substantial advertising entrance fee and subscription, new brands will not succeed in entering the club. Advertising is inseparable from efficient competition.

There may seem at first sight to be a paradox between the two findings just quoted: the PIMS data saying that larger brands have larger advertising to sales ratios, the Jones diagram that larger brands have a lower Share of Voice than they have Share of Market. A little thought will show that the two findings are, in fact, consistent. There are relatively few large brands in any market. A brand leader with, say, a 30% A:S ratio could well have a below average share of total *advertising* spend if there are, say, five other smaller brands with 15% A:S ratios. New launches, where the brand is seeking to stimulate volume growth, often have a Share of Voice much larger than their Share of Market (Broadbent[18])

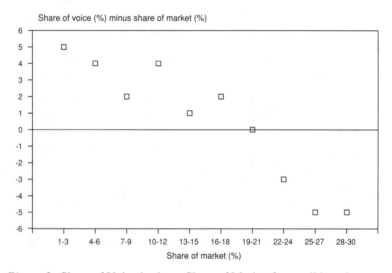

Figure 3. Share of Voice is above Share of Market for small brands, below Share of Market for large brands.
Source: Jones (1988)

3. *Advertising makes it easier for established players in a market to introduce new brands and varieties*. Jones[57] quotes a number of studies showing a tendency for markets to fragment with increasing numbers of brands; at the same time, the evidence suggests that the concentration of *firms* within markets remains stable over time. The clear inference is that most of the attempts at innovation in a market, whether

successful or not, come from existing manufacturers in the market, who are able to benefit from scale economies in production, R&D, sales force employment etc. Thus the companies already in the market tend to maintain their overall share, even if that is divided differently between brands. The evidence suggests that there is little if any relationship between the concentration ratios of companies and advertising[74, 75, 31].

Evidence from the PIMS database, referred to earlier, showed that advertisers who either cut their budgets in the recession, or increased them by only a modest amount, lost ROI and made only small gains in market share; but the small minority of companies who increased their advertising by about 50% were able to gain a full point in market share, at the cost of a larger temporary reduction in ROI. Obviously, it will tend to be the larger and stronger brands which have the financial base to ride through a recession in this aggressive way (Biel[7,10]).

4. *Advertising stimulates a reduction in retailers' margins*, and thus contributes to reducing consumer prices. This surprising finding has become known as the Steiner Effect, since it was reported by Robert Steiner in a paper on the toy market in 1973[102]; it has been confirmed on a much wider scale by Reekie[94]. What appears to happen is that because consumers are familiar with the prices of advertised brands, retailers are unable to vary prices, and the cheapest price tends to become the norm. Because advertising makes the selling job easier, a lower margin is less of a problem for the retailer. In this way, advertising increases the elasticity of demand to the retailer at the same time as it reduces it to the manufacturer. The upward pressure on the manufacturer's price that advertising encourages by brand differentiation is counteracted, not only by competition, but by a downward pressure on

retailers' margins.

Concentration among retailers, unlike manufacturers, appears to be increasing. It is not clear what effect this has on the Steiner Effect. Greater retailer power may tend to push up margins (hence the rise in promotional expenditures); on the other hand, it is argued that the stronger brands, which are also the most heavily advertised ones, are the very ones which the retail trade cannot afford to lose; it is therefore dangerous for them to try to increase their margins on these.

5. *The long-term effect on price.* To sum up the argument so far:

   • Advertising, by branding, increases demand and creates the conditions for a higher price which consumers may be willing to pay.
   • Competition sucks in an increase in supply and stimulates a search for greater efficiency and reduction of costs: this enables prices to reduce. The equilibrium settles at a new, lower price level.

Jones[57] quotes evidence from Unilever showing that, after adjusting for inflation, 22 major brands from that company across the world had prices lower in 1957 than they had been in 1938. Competition and scale economies contribute to price reductions in real terms which can be passed on to the consumer. On the other hand, branding justifies premium prices, as shown by comparison with generics and by other evidence (eg Jones[58]). Other evidence that advertising tends to keep prices down is given by King[66], from two studies which compared heavily advertised food brands against the Retail Price Index for all food. Out of 25 categories of branded food, *all* brands were listed which had both been on the market for ten years and had spent at least £50,000 on advertising in 1964. Taking 1955 as the base year (= 100), the index of prices for these 78 heavily advertised brands rose to 114 in 1965; but the index for all foods rose to 130 in the same period. The analysis was repeated, covering the years from 1964 to 1978: this time, all food brands were listed which had spent over £¼ million on advertising in 1977 and were on sale during the whole period. With 1964 as base, the index for the 67 heavily advertised brands rose to 311 in 1978, compared to 408 for the entire food Retail Price Index.

Jones[57] identifies five factors relating advertising to price: two of these push prices up, two bring them down, and the fifth provides an indirect benefit. The factors increasing prices are the cost of the advertising (typically 4-8% of net sales value, which increases consumer prices by about 5%), and the power of branding to command a price premium. The factors reducing prices are the downward pressure over the long term due to scale economies in addition to the effects of competition (this reduction could be, he estimates, of the order of 10% for large volume packaged goods, but has been very much greater for some technically-oriented products, eg pocket calculators), and the reduction in retail margins through the Steiner Effect (which probably accounts for at least 5% reduction). The fifth factor, which provides an indirect benefit, is the very large subsidy paid by advertising to the media, which greatly reduces media costs to consumers.

Summary: effects of advertising on markets and brands

The discussion in this section has reviewed the evidence enabling us to place advertising as a factor in the economy and the operation of markets.

1. It appears, from the very limited circumstantial evidence available, that advertising does not often lead in creating overall demand for a product or service. Advertising affects brands within markets; at the 'market' level, demand grows, stabilises or declines for other reasons.

2. Many markets in developed economies, especially packaged goods (FMCG) markets, are 'mature' in that the population's capacity to absorb greater usage is saturated. Advertising can do little to increase demand in such cases; nor can it do much to reduce demand for a product thought to be undesirable if that demand is firmly established.

3. Advertising's role is much less to create demand than to show people how to satisfy the demands they have. It does this by fuelling the competition between brands in a market, helping to establish and formulate the differentiation which defines the brands (added values). Advertising's main economic function can thus be seen as the lubrication of competition.

4. Markets have either reached or are tending towards equilibrium, in which a limited number of competing firms acquire and maintain brand shares based on the differentiated branding they have achieved. When a market has settled down into such a pattern, the stability is maintained by the natural inertia of consumer habits, as revealed by what we know of purchasing behaviour, especially from Ehrenberg's work. The equilibrium is, however, a *dynamic tension* rather than a static condition; there may be frequent oscillations around the stable state, under the influence of brand or product innovation and aggressive competition, and such movements may well lead to long-term changes in the relative positioning of brands. Advertising is involved both in

disturbing the equilibrium and maintaining it.

5. A brand which achieves a high share of a market can benefit from economies of scale: it can afford to spend more, but needs to invest relatively less compared to its smaller competitors, to maintain its position. By the same token, new brands fighting for share against established competitors have to pay a high premium, and easily fail. Advertising can achieve more with less effort if there is a past success in branding to build upon.

6. Advertising influences the effective price (the price which can be charged to yield a given level of sales) in two ways: upward, by branding which justifies a price premium that consumers are willing to pay, and downward, by fuelling competition, through the economies of scale possible from successful branding, and through the downward pressure which a large brand can exert on retailer margins. The evidence is that the more the competition, and the more consumers are informed of it through advertising, the lower prices are likely to be.

4 Sales effectiveness of advertising

Advertising has been shown to have its effect at the level of the individual brand, enabling it to become established and to compete. We must now proceed to look at the detail of this effect on brands, starting at the point where it must ultimately be held accountable: sales. How can we establish *what* effect advertising has on its ultimate objective? This is not, as it may seem at first sight, a deviation from the question of how advertising works to a different question, how to measure it. Our understanding of advertising, and of its value in marketing, is in fact crucially coloured by our perceptions about the possibility of measuring its effect on sales.

Most advertising is intended to increase, or maintain, sales in some form. There is of course a very wide range, from the frequent and trivial purchase cycle to the rare and expensive, even one-off, purchase which requires a serious decision. Some advertising, also, is aimed at changing or maintaining an attitude or culture to provide a context in which a desired behaviour is more likely to take place: corporate advertising is like that, and so is much public advertising (eg for wearing seat-belts, or anti drink/drive). These differences affect the ease with which one can measure sales, if they are appropriate to measure at all. But even though they may require different methods, many of the principles we are about to discuss apply across all the variations.

One qualification should be made here. It is tempting, and commonly done, to think of 'sales' in purely volume terms and of sales success as shifting more poundage or collecting more revenue. In fact, in most markets, the relationship between volume and price, the 'demand curve' referred to in the previous section, is what is important. The aim is to shift the demand curve to the right, so that, while the relationship remains the same, either the same price yields greater volume, or the same volume is sold at a higher price, both desirable outcomes. In what follows, 'sales' will be used as a shorthand for 'effective sales', or the 'sales-price relationship'.

Long-term and short-term effects

As we have seen, advertising is an instrument for *branding*, the differentiation which distinguishes one product in the field from another and enables it to arrive at its market share. This inevitably imposes a long-term view; successful brands go on for years, sometimes it seems for ever; advertising is a continuing investment. On the other hand, an individual advertisement is a fleeting event, quickly forgotten, although sometimes messages from it, especially if repeated, may stick in the mind for a long time. Also, we know that sometimes, when conditions are right, we can observe changes in sales following a burst of advertising which cannot be explained by anything else, so that there must be a short-term response.

Are they really different?

Commentators have commonly written about short- and long-term effects as conceptually quite distinct. Jones[61], for example, writes as follows:

'I believe that advertising works by stimulating sales in the short-term. This stimulates brand purchase by consumers, brand use, and the long-term buildup of added values which stems from brand use. Thus the long-term effect of advertising is via long-term use of the brand and not so much the advertising itself.'

And Corlett[26]:

'It is generally accepted that the effects of advertising on the sales of a brand are of at least two distinct kinds – a *long-term* effect which contributes to and helps to sustain the "saleability" of the brand (its image and priceworthiness in the eyes of consumers) and a *short-term* effect which exploits this "saleability" by stimulating additional sales in the short term.'

'Saleability' was a term originally coined by Grahame Leman in a paper entitled 'Sales, saleability and the saleability gap', published in 1969[77], in which he argued against the danger of concentrating too much on short-term promotion at the expense of advertising investment: the term was taken up by later writers as a more accurate shorthand expression of a difficult idea. 'Saleability' is clearly closely related to 'added values', although not identical in meaning.

These quotations give the flavour of what must be the prevailing view among practitioners. However, it is often quoted somewhat defensively. It is clear that some people, including some managers involved with setting advertising budgets, find it difficult to look beyond the short-term. This can lead them, dangerously (Broadbent[18]), to cut advertising where it appears, as is often the case, a relatively inefficient way of stimulating short-term sales, compared to in-store promotions.

Sales measures short-term by definition

The underlying problem is that virtually all the methods now available for measuring and attributing sales variations to advertising are only possible short-term. These methods, especially econometrics, are in regular use by sophisticated managements and are discussed more fully below. In the longer term, advertising becomes lost in other influences; its effects are indirect and inferential. The brand's image (its perceived 'added values') is the necessary background against which choices are made, but it is something in the mind, fed only partly by advertising and more importantly by satisfactory experience of the brand itself living up to its promise. In the first five volumes of IPA Advertising Effectiveness Awards[50-54], the demonstrations offered of advertising affecting sales were all short-term; for the sixth year[55], the organisers deliberately included a category entitled 'longer and broader' in an attempt to plug this gap. The ensuing publication included a number of very convincing demonstrations of the practical value of a long-term advertising investment, headed by the amazing case of the PG Tips chimps[24].

A muddled argument

For these reasons the tendency to think and write of long and short-term effects as two quite different things is under-standable. It has, however, led to some very strange muddles. Derek Bloom and Michael Stewart, for example, have argued that only short-term effects should or need be considered, either in measurement or for setting budgets, on the ground that it is meaningless to impute to an advertisement now a delayed action which will only be realised in an unquantifiable way some unknown time in the future. Bloom puts it thus:

'On the whole, one has to be agnostic about whether there are long-run *sales* effects from advertising, since it is not necessary to assume them to explain what goes on in the market place.

Certainly it is difficult to accept a 'time-bomb' effect in which an advertisement now – barely noticed by the television viewer or magazine reader, probably forgotten in any conscious sense within a very short time even if it is noticed, and supposedly having no effect on her pro-pensity to purchase on the next occasion that she buys in that product group – can nevertheless 'explode' 18 months or three years from now so as to induce a sale that otherwise would not have taken place.' (Bloom[11])

Stewart[103] argues that econometric analysis will estimate diminishing returns progressing some way into the future, but would underestimate long-term effects if they were assumed to be large. Bloom returned to the attack in 1989: 'It takes a certain hardihood of spirit to contemplate an advertising half-life of twenty years or more.'[12]

These arguments aroused fury from the believers in long-term effects, brand building and saleability. But in their own terms they are correct. Nobody actually believes the *reductio ad absurdum* in the above quotation. The supporters of long-term effects are thinking of something quite different from the target shot at by Stewart and Bloom. They have not always helped themselves, however, by making it clear what they do think it is. For example, Corlett again:

'The evidence for the existence of *long-term* effects is derived mainly from "case studies" but the evidence from such studies, however convincing, is usually general rather than specific and is often difficult to translate into the quantified terms ideally required for budget-setting.'[26]

And Baker[4]:

'I believe that it is *impossible to quantify* longer-term effects of advertising with any confidence. Because of this, *wrongly*, longer-term effects are often completely ignored in an evaluation, being assumed to be some sort of "invisible bonus" which automatically accrues whatever the advertising... What we can do is monitor brand standing – in general terms, and ideally against specific (long-term) objectives that have been set.'

Comments like these can be read, perhaps unfairly, as arguing on Bloom's ground: advertising now does have some sort of effect into the future, but we can't fix what it is.

The advertising continuum

It would be helpful, I suggest, to abandon the terminology of long- and short-term, which by now has made its point and is adding nothing new to our understanding. A better approach is to think of advertising effect as a *continuum*. After a new brand has grown (which we are often able to relate relatively easily to the advertising), it reaches a stable share; thereafter, advertising's main function is to maintain that share against competition. This is an on-going process. It often fluctuates with discontinuous bursts, which may stimulate immediate responses which fall away again; but any period we look at, short or long, is part of a length of string which goes back to the start of the brand and continues on indefinitely into the future. Seen in this way, *there is no difference between short- and long-term effects*: they are different aspects of the same process. Each advertisement seen, if it works at all, stimulates its immediate response: the continuum, however far into the future, is merely the continued repetition of such responses.

This way of thinking is well supported by 'The Andrex story[56]', one of the case histories published by the IPA in *Advertising Works*, vol 4[53]. Andrex is the leading brand of toilet tissue in the UK, a position which Bowater Scott have used consistent advertising to maintain. To demonstrate the effect of advertising over time, the team at JWT modelled Andrex sales through 22 years. Advertising was shown to have a short-term elasticity of 0.06 (see note on p.27). The longer-term effect of advertising 'takes its particular shape from the carry-over value of 61 per cent. This means that 61 per cent of sales generated by advertising in a period continue into the next period, and 61 per cent of that amount continue into the next and so on.' This very high level of carry-over of 61 per cent is based on comparisons between quarterly periods, during which there were on average eight to ten purchases of the product per period, so that it appears convincing that this is genuine retention: competitive influences were not sufficient to lure recent Andrex buyers away, at least not rapidly. The authors believed that this high retention level could be attributed in part to the practice of advertising Andrex continuously, rather than in bursts; but they also make this comment:

'We do not suppose that this long-term effect is achieved through memory of specific periods of advertising; simply that the purchase and use of Andrex, once adopted, is slow to fall away. It is the behaviour that echoes through time. Such persistence of behaviour must reflect the actual quality of the Andrex product as well as the added values of the Andrex brand personality.'

This precisely expresses what we mean by a continuum, where what happens now rests on what has gone before and carries forward to the future.

It is worth noting here that all four of the case histories published under the heading of 'Longer and Broader Effects' in IPA *Advertising Works*, Vol 6[55], attributed their success in part to the *consistency* with which they had maintained their advertising over time. The brands were PG Tips, Croft Original, Silentnight and Champagne Lanson. In the PG Tips case it was said that: 'If the paper has shown nothing else, it has shown that *consistency* in a strong creative vehicle and at high levels of media weight can ensure the brand does indeed become invested with added value and can pay back dramatically over the long term …The declining fortunes of each of these (competitive) brands correlates …with a strategy of *chopping and changing the content* of the advertising and with *lower support* for the advertising.'[24]

Metaphors to help clarify the 'advertising continuum'

Simon Broadbent[18] uses a striking metaphor to represent this idea of a continuum. The sales of a brand are like the height at which an aeroplane flies (they climb at first, then level out). 'Advertising spend is like its engines: while the engines are running, everything is fine but, when the engines stop, the descent starts. The effectiveness of branding is like the aerodynamic design of the plane. Great creative, or better design, means that by spending the same money, or by using the same engines, we take the brand or the plane higher. If we cut spending on advertising, or stop the engines, the better brand or plane will stay up longer. But both will come down! Note that, in this analogy, advertising both creates increases in sales (gets the plane up) and is needed to maintain sales (to stay at the same height is an achievement).'

This illuminating metaphor clarifies two things: what advertising does, short- or long-term, is the same (each rev of the engine is just a unit in the total running time, but not different in kind), and the crucial importance of seeing advertising, not in isolation or in separate periods, but as part of a continuing operation. Broadbent argues for the importance of advertising's contribution to the *base* (the level of sales already reached, the height at which the plane is flying): he quotes with approval King (from a paper given at a Market Research Society Seminar, 'The Proof of Advertising Value', in 1976): 'It's possible by confining ourselves to short-term measures to over-estimate the importance of something affecting the variations from a norm or base, and under-estimate the importance of what has affected the size of the base.'

No analogy is ever quite complete, however, and it might fill out the picture if we add some other images. We might, for example, think of the brand as a sea wall, built in the past to protect against erosion of the coastline. It is under constant attack from the sea, which tends to keep breaking it down; sometimes there are storms (competition) which breach it and wash away the stones. It has to be kept under constant repair. Advertising is the new stones and mortar which must constantly be added; sometimes, when we are expecting a severe storm, we put in extra funds to shore up the wall in advance. Each new stone has a function no different in kind from all the other stones. Hedges[45] saw the effect in similar terms as 'sedimentary': deposits left by successive grains of sand.

Alternatively, if that is too static an image, try this: brands competing in a market are like stags at mating time. They rush together and lock antlers, and push each other backwards and forwards over the same territory as each tries to seek a foothold and gain ground from the other. But because they are equally matched, neither gains in the long-term (the system returns to equilibrium), although sometimes one may, after a long fight, manage to keep an advantage it has gained. Advertising is what provides the energy which each stag expends in the battle. Although there may be an overall tendency to equilibrium, what is happening on the ground can be highly dramatic. Advertising can easily gain a sudden advantage, and it may take time before the opposition summons up the energy to counteract it. On this analogy, the status quo in the market is maintained, but with an *effort*. By advertising, a brand keeps or gains small bits of ground; but if advertising stops altogether, the brand will fall right off the mountain. The one certain thing about a stag fight is that the stag that stops fighting first will be beaten.

The importance of maintaining the base

If the central idea in these imperfect analogies is accepted, it gets us off the hook of defining long-term effects. They can be more easily understood as the continuous process of maintaining the base appropriate for the brand. The immediate, or short-term, effects are part of this continuum; they prevent erosion of the base, and carry it on into the future. The advertiser's task is to understand that base (why we are where we are), and decide whether we want to stay there or attempt to change it in some way. Proposed campaigns can then be judged in terms of their capacity to maintain, or develop, the base as required.

Why is this concept of the base important? Because increasingly companies have come to rely on short-term volume changes in sales to evaluate advertising effect, following the availability of econometrics and other methods and the continued lack of clarity about the supposed long-term. As a result, to quote Broadbent: 'many managements now believe that these blips are all advertising does'[18]. But, very often, advertising is a relatively inefficient and expensive way of achieving a short-term sales increase. If managers and their accountants take the view that all advertising is for is to 'move more boxes off shelves' and has nothing to do with the reason why sales have achieved their present level, the pressure to cut it and boost the bottom line for this year may be irresistible. Such attitudes follow naturally from the obsession with volume sales and market share noted by Jones[60] as a consequence of market maturation.

As Broadbent has shown in his 'Death of a Brand' example[18], they are also highly dangerous. In this case, the short-term advertising effect, as econometrically modelled, was below breakeven (which is quite normal), and the decision was taken to cut the advertising and lower the price, which, it was calculated, would return a larger profit. For six months it worked: the aeroplane stayed up, and the planned profit was delivered. But within a year the brand's share started to decline. Within two years it was so low that the brand was withdrawn. The post-mortem showed that the company had failed to realise how the advertising supported the value of the brand. Retailers and sales staff lost confidence in it; the price reduction meant lower profits for retailers (without any compensation in higher volume through perceived value), and distribution dropped.

Pedigree Petfoods is a regular and substantial advertiser, as a long-term investment. Laurence Hazelhurst, their Media Controller, wrote in 1988:

'Typical comments about the effectiveness of advertising which I often hear from media owners are "advertising shifts product" or "advertising stimulates sales"

'Both statements imply that advertising should be used for a sales boost, to run down stocks, as a quick way of generating sales. In fact it is a very expensive way of doing that. For example, even on a medium-sized brand of around £20 million per annum turnover, a simple calculation would show that you would need a large sustained uplift in sales, and a big margin, to justify say a £1 million network TV burst of a few months. There are, in fact, far more effective ways of boosting volume in the short-term, such as: price promotions, instore feature/display, retail outlet led promotions. A more appropriate statement of the above about advertising might be "advertising shifts money" – fast.'[44]

Jones, in *Does it pay to advertise?*, a collection of American and British case histories[58], speaks of advertising having an immediate and also a lagged effect: all advertising which is effective achieves both. The 'lagged' effect (not perhaps the best term, if one follows the idea of a continuum) is 'another way of saying that it builds added values, which... operate in conjunction with consumer satisfaction with a brand's functional properties to ensure repeat purchase of the brand in a competitive marketplace.' In some cases, this effect acts over time, not so much to increase penetration by converting people, but rather to strengthen and develop the attitudes of those who already use the brand:

> 'Modification of attitudes does not mean a reversal of what people feel about a brand at the moment; it means a process of modest adaptation or fine-tuning, if possible by building on strengths and correcting weaknesses.
>
> In this book, two major cases describe such a modification of attitudes. With the Trustee Savings Bank, success was achieved, but it took almost a decade of consistent effort to bring it about; with Goodyear, progress has been made with a campaign that has run for four years, but the path yet to be travelled is greater than the distance already covered. The slow but continuous influence of advertising on users of a brand is "one of the reasons that campaigns can have long lives." '[58]

This concept of an immediate and 'lagged' effect is entirely consistent with saying that the long- and the short-term effects of advertising are not two different things, but rather different aspects of the same thing. Both operate now, with each exposure which is attended to. If change occurs (or resistance is strengthened) over time, it is not something booked forward in the future, but the slow accretion of each instant on those that have gone before. Change occurs when, brick by brick, we do not merely repair the sea wall but actually raise it a little higher.

Short-term measurements of sales effects

There are several published examples now which have been able to show a short-term sales effect convincingly attributable to advertising. A number are contained in the six volumes of *Advertising Works*[50-55]. They have increasingly used methods which new data collecting technology and computer power have made available; in particular, we shall discuss econometrics, single-source data, and the use of either of these in controlled experiments. The important point to realise is that these cases only confirm the *possibility* of showing sales effects. There are also many published examples which have failed to show effects at all, and no doubt the same applies to the legion which remain unpublished.

Econometrics

The main reason why it is difficult to relate changes in sales, assuming they can be observed at all, to advertising is that there are so many other factors involved, both on the side of the advertiser (promotions, price, distribution etc) and from other players (retailers, competitors). It is hard to disentangle these influences. Until the emergence of econometrics, marketers tended to rely on measures of response where the relationship with advertising can be traced more directly, such as brand or advertising awareness; many still do. These substitute measures are in no sense equivalent to sales, but they can be evidence that the advertising is at least being noticed.

Econometrics are a set of mathematical techniques designed to achieve the 'disentangling' of the different influences on sales and partition the observed variations in sales between them. The first point to realise is that they are just that – techniques – and do not imply any theory about how advertising and other factors affect sales. The operation depends crucially on our judgement in the first place about what variables might affect sales, and how we should define them. In studying any particular market, there is always a certain amount of trial and error while the analysts work out the best formulations for explaining the actual data.

The essential idea of econometrics has been well described in layman's terms by writers such as Corlett[25,27], Stewart[103] and

Oherlihy (several articles since 1976[89]). The first step is to draw up a list of all the variables which we think might affect the sales of our brand: not only advertising, but promotions, price, competitors' prices, seasonal factors such as temperature, etc. These explanatory variables are fed into a statistical process known as 'multiple regression', the aim of which is to produce a model of the following form:

$$\text{Sales} = a \text{ (a constant)} + b \times (\text{price}) + c \times (\text{temperature}) + d \times \ldots\text{etc.}$$

The letters b, c, d, etc, represent *weights* which are applied to each explanatory variable. The model works out the set of weights which gives the closest fit to the actual movements in sales, ie, the estimate which leaves the least amount unexplained. The computer not only tells you the values of the weights, but how close a fit the model is. You inspect this evidence to see whether the relative weights given to the explanatory variables makes sense and whether they account for the sales data accurately and credibly enough; if not, you try again with a different formulation. Normally, it may require several attempts before we have a satisfactory model.

This account makes clear that the modelling process is, above all else, a system for testing out assumptions. It is always the user who specifies the form of the relationship, the value of which is then estimated from the data. It should be done in a scientific manner, in which different hypotheses are put forward, tested rigorously, and progressively revised[89].

Adstock: estimating rates of decay

Where advertising is concerned, an important set of assumptions which have to be explicitly taken into account concerns the rate at which immediate or short-term effects decay. Advertising is usually put into these models in terms of weight (usually television ratings (TVRs), ie, the proportion having an 'opportunity to see' a commercial during a certain period; since the bulk of advertising spend is on television, if other media are involved, the spend is converted into TVR equivalents). A single advertisement exposure, if effective at all, is expected to have only a transitory effect on response; a burst of advertising may bump up sales, but when that burst ceases the sales are likely to fall back again after a while towards their equilibrium, until they receive another stimulus. We need a way of formulating the rate at which the resulting response to an advertisement decays over time until a new stimulus occurs. The method for doing this is now known generally as 'adstock' (Broadbent[14]). The adstock in a period is a rearrangement of TVRs in such a way that the progressively decayed values of TVRs from previous periods are taken into account as well as the current values of the TVRs in this period; it is assumed, in other words, that TVRs do not have the whole of their effect immediately, but that it carries on at a diminishing rate into the future. The decay rates are modelled using the principle of the 'half-life' drawn from atomic physics; the actual values are those estimated from actual data to give the best fit. When adstock has been calculated satisfactorily, that is what goes into the econometric model, replacing raw advertising weights.

Uses and limitations of econometrics

Econometric modelling helps to clarify understanding of the reasons why sales may have moved as they did during a recent period (what hypothesis should we accept?), and enable marketing managements to try out 'what if?' scenarios, if some of the weights were changed in future. It is thus a useful operating tool. But it has a number of well-recognised limitations, which mean that it must be used with caution and judgement.

One obvious limitation is that there must be some variation: sales must actually move up and down a bit during the period studied, or there will be nothing to explain. The same applies to advertising and the other explanatory variables. If advertising is at a *continuous* rate, rather than in bursts, it will not appear as an important explanatory variable in the model. There can be serious danger that this will lead to a management under-valuing its true contribution in keeping sales at a consistent level.

Following from this last point, econometrics has little to say about the effects of advertising over long periods of time, simply because sales variations tend to be short in duration. 'Econometrics ... by putting a figure on the advertising effect which is necessarily derived from the short-term fluctuation of sales ... creates the illusion that the effects of sustained, defensive advertising over long periods of time do not have any real existence.' (Feldwick[36]).

A second general point, already discussed, is that the outcome of any model depends crucially on the assumptions governing the selection of variables put into it, and must always be tested against common sense and judgement, never treated as gospel.

Independence, interaction, and cause and effect

There is another point, which has been somewhat less noticed. Econometric modelling works by *separating out* the contribution made by each explanatory variable. There is *in the technique* an inbuilt assumption of independence; we detect how much of the variation we can attribute to advertising, how much to promotion, etc, and *add* them together. One of the problems the technique has to surmount is that, in fact, there is often correlation; for example, advertising and a price cut might occur at the same time – which of them, we ask, is responsible for the effect observed? This has always been recognised by practitioners, and sophisticated methods have been developed to overcome it.

But why should we assume that these influences are independent? They are, in real life, just as likely to be *inter*dependent; indeed, that is often the intention behind the planning of the marketing mix. Advertising and promotions in-store, for example, may be deliberately timed to coincide, so as to improve receptiveness in the trade and alert consumers. Even if not planned, interaction is at least as probable as independence. And, if this is true, there is a serious danger, as Broadbent argues[18], that the true effect of advertising will be underestimated, because we are only observing what is unequivocally attributable to it. Strictly, to overcome this difficulty, we should be feeding into our econometric models not separate but composite variables: advertising plus promotion, etc, as well as advertising on its own. It is easy to see that the resulting matrices would become very complicated and would put a strain on data collection, if not computing power.

I believe that underlying this difficulty there is a deeper problem. We have been very much conditioned by traditional notions of causal inference. Although cause and effect can never be logically proved, it can be convincingly inferred if we are able to show that the effect occurs when, and only when, the 'cause' has been present beforehand. But, if two potential causes are present at the same time, we are stymied. We fall into the trap of thinking that there has to be *a* cause, we can't say which it is, therefore neither counts. Underlying this again is the unspoken mental picture that 'causes' are active and 'effects' passive and inert, like billiard balls being struck by other billiard balls. Something called 'advertising' acts upon something called 'sales', so as to bring about a change. The quantified artifacts (TVRs, etc) we feed into the models easily encourage this kind of simplified thinking. But, as we shall see later, it does not fit the real situation in which people choose. In reality, it is the other way round: the potential 'causes' are alternatives presented for choice, the 'effects' buyers actively exercising their choice. So the question is not so much 'what has caused the sales of A to rise?' as 'what has increased the probability of buyers choosing A instead of B?' It seems compelling that buyers would be more likely to choose A if A is both advertised and promoted than if it were only one or the other, and that the effect might well be a multiple.

This is not an argument against econometrics, but merely a plea for sensitivity in selecting and interpreting the variables we put into them, and being aware of the assumptions we have to make.

What explains sales?

We have already referred to the concept of the 'base', the level of sales, market share, brand equity etc which has already been achieved by previous marketing and which current advertising keeps in being. Short-term measures of sales effects are, by definition, fluctuations about this base: they are incremental (or decremental) only. This has naturally led econometric modellers to see the 'base' and the incremental movements as different components, only the latter of which is explained by advertising and promotional spends at local points in time. The 'base' is then treated as a separate constant, a carry-over sales effect, although it is recognised that it is capable of rising or falling over time. This separation of the 'base' and the increment is another aspect of the tendency to see long- and short-term effects as two different things.

The idea that there is a large component of a brand's sales which is somehow self-explanatory, like a car without a driver, is conceptually awkward, and Broadbent[16] has shown that it is difficult for the modellers to cope with mathematically: for example, it is possible to model the same data to show a large incremental effect and a small effect on the base, or, conversely, a small increment and a large effect on the base; these are mathematical artefacts, but the implications for promotional budgets of choosing one over the other could be considerable. In a recent paper[15], Broadbent proposes a different approach to the understanding of sales, which abolishes this confusing distinction between 'base' and 'increment'. In this system, the effects on sales of price and distribution are identified and allowed for, and the residual remaining is, for want of a better word, the 'consumer brand equity' (Broadbent comments that this term 'has nothing to do with an accountant's valuation … We might say "strength" or "value" or "power", but "equity" seems to have stuck and "consumer" emphasises where our data have come from.') The definition of equity is 'the sales share we would get if we were at average price and had average distribution – and average price and distribution elasticities applied.'

Broadbent emphasises that this 'equity' is not necessarily to be taken as the long-term effect of advertising: many other things which go on in the marketplace may cause it to change. But, sometimes at least, 'when we have examined all the possibilities, the point which may emerge is that the brands with high or growing equity are those with good advertising weight and what we judge to be relevant and persuasive advertising copy.' The main point is that it is a clearer way of expressing sales, looking at averages and trends rather than temporary 'blips', as a simple combination of price, distribution and everything else that has combined to give the brand its franchise, including all that has happened in the past.

Experiments

If it is possible to control variables, so that advertising at different times or in different areas is present at different weights (or absent altogether) whilst the other possible influences are unchanged, one can have greater confidence in attributing sales variations to the only variable which changes. It can, unfortunately, be very difficult to set up such controlled experiments to be sure that there are no hidden factors, or that they are not spoilt by deliberate competitive tactics. The best known experimental modelling system, which has been widely publicised, is Beecham's AMTES, which works by comparing what happened in the test area with what would have happened if the advertising had not taken place; ideally, this is calculated from another control area, similar in other ways as far as possible: sales in the preceding period are compared to establish how they relate, and one then sees if during the test period the two areas diverge.

Single-source data

One of the problems with econometrics is that the information we feed into the models is itself of a very summary kind – amounts spent, sales revenues received, etc – and depends on how we choose to define it. We are not working at the level of real consumer responses, and therefore our inferences about relationships are still several removes from reality.

Problems with panels

It has already been noted that most of what we actually *know* about consumer purchasing behaviour comes from the work of Ehrenberg and his colleagues, based on *purchasing panels*. These are continuous records of purchases kept by the same individuals (or households) over long periods of time. Such panels have been a major source of research information for large FMCG companies for at least forty years, and their value for describing how purchasing patterns are distributed has been considerable. They are, however, expensive to run, and until recent years have suffered from two drawbacks which particularly concern us: the methods of data collection, usually paper diaries, imposed a heavy load on informants, and caused problems in keeping up their enthusiasm and accuracy; more importantly, it was impossible to collect details of media exposure, and therefore possible exposure to advertising, from the same people as their purchasing data over time, and therefore any attempt to link the two involved difficult and imprecise inferences, subject to sampling errors between different sets of people.

Effects of new technology

Both these difficulties disappeared with the appearance of some clever new technology. On the one hand, broadcast meters were invented for use in the audience research business; these, attached to a television set, could record minute by minute whether the set was on and what channel it was tuned to, and transmit the data automatically by phone to a central computer without involving family members. More recent developments can identify who is watching, recording and playback on video, etc. On the other hand, the invention of bar-code scanners and electronic point of sale (EPOS) recording meant that selected panels of people could have all their purchase details identified and recorded on each occasion, again without involving them in any troublesome task; either it is done at the shop till, or they have a hand-held device which they sweep over the bar-coded product at home, the data being recorded automatically and plugged into the main computer via the telephone line.

These two technical developments together solved the panel problem: it would now be possible to obtain measurements over time, painlessly from the same individuals, of their purchase records day by day and their opportunities to be exposed to advertising daily (for press), minute by minute (for broadcast media), together with other relevant detail attached to purchases, such as price and promotions. The only deterrent was the high capital investment cost of the equipment and the need to ensure that all stores in the neighbourhood of a panel are covered; in practice this has meant that the main development has been in the USA, where geographical separation of markets makes it relatively easy to set up segregated test areas. It was widely expected that the data produced would be the ultimate data for understanding how advertising works. 'Using such information (UPC scanner data) together with an accurate record of advertising exposures to the same consumers over time, it would be highly probable that much better individual brand optimal frequency data could be generated, and at an affordable cost.' (Naples[85]).

Single-source development in the USA

The leaders in the single-source field have been Information Resources Inc (IRI), with a system named BehaviorScan. They, from the beginning, followed the line of setting up experimental test markets. They would take a geographical market with a cable television facility, ensure that all stores in the market were equipped with their scanners, and set up panels receiving cable TV. For any test, the panel could be split into subsamples precisely matched in terms of their purchasing patterns in the relevant product field: equal proportions of solus buyers, frequent and infrequent buyers, buyers from different stores exposed to different deals, etc. It would then be possible to control what each sample received in TV advertising through the cable network, and vary the brand which was to be tested while keeping other stimuli the same. These would typically be weight tests or tests of new copy executions. Press advertising could also be controlled between the samples in a similar way, with a little effort. The normal practice for such tests is to run both subsamples for a period beforehand, and then to see how their buying patterns diverge when the test starts; because the panels are continuous, it is also possible to continue the measurement for some time after the end of the advertising test to see how long sales, if increased, stay up.

A major reason why IRI have confined their measurements of advertising effectiveness to matched sample tests with controlled delivery of commercials is that in the USA, unlike Britain, there is no organisation which regularly monitors which commercials are transmitted in each slot (it would, of course, be much harder to achieve this in America, because of the multiplicity of geographical markets and channels). As we shall explain below, this has limited their ability to exploit the power of single-source data as they might have done. However, this could now change. IRI have announced[48] a joint licensing agreement with Arbitron, which will enable the IRI national product scanning service, Infoscan, to combine with Arbitron's television viewing and monitoring data: this, we understand, is capable of identifying transmissions by pattern recognition. There is also now a competing national service, Nielsen's HomeScan[87]; this also can identify transmissions through a computerised pattern recognition system, but, unlike IRI, collects purchase data from its panel using hand-held scanners in the home; these scanners not only read bar-codes on products bought, but also record recent reading events, again by scanning bar-codes attached to magazine titles[62]. Thus, for the first time, there is the prospect of two genuine national single-source panel services in the United States, with different methodologies for collecting product purchasing and media exposure data from their panel members.

Findings from BehaviorScan tests

Tests on the BehaviorScan system have now been carried out for some years. IRI have issued[49] a report on a review of nearly 400 tests, in which account was taken, not only of the test results themselves, but also of the advertising objectives as revealed by the advertisers and their agencies to the investigators. What have these findings shown?

As with econometric and other studies, the results have been equivocal: sometimes there has been a short-term sales effect, but just as often there has not. Results which have been reported in November 1991[49] and in earlier articles can be summarised as follows.

1. *About half of advertising weight tests show an increase in sales, the other half do not.* Out of 293 weight tests carried out by IRI in the USA between 1984 and 1988, 49% resulted in an increase[1,2]. 40 tests in Germany, from the GfK test site in Hassloch which uses BehaviorScan methodology, yielded a similar figure, 55% showing a sales increase (Litzenroth[78]). Such proportions are no different from what one would expect by chance, tossing a coin.

2. *The same applies to copy tests.* There appeared to be no clear relationship between copy test scores, whether obtained by recall or persuasion, and test results. This raises other issues, which will be returned to later.

3. *New product advertising yielded sales increases more frequently than established brands.* In the USA, 58% of the new brands tested showed a sales increase attributable to the advertising, but only 46% of the established brands. The equivalent figures in Germany were 57% and 50%. The average sales increases, where they occur, are higher for new brands (about 23%) than for established brands (about 10%). Similarly, BehaviorScan copy tests for new brands predicted 'success' in 70% of cases compared to only 31% for established brands[1,2,79,80].
We would have expected this finding on theoretical grounds already discussed: established brands tend to have reached equilibrium shares. The disturbing thing about the figures is not that new brands have a higher 'success' rate, but rather that *even then* there is still so high a proportion of 'failures'.

4. When advertising does show an effect, it occurs rapidly; new

sales above the existing trend start to show within six months. Conversely, if there is no effect within six months, there continues to be no effect even if the test is continued for a year. This applies both to weight change and copy change tests. It strongly confirms our belief, already stated, that advertising which works does so immediately.

5. For some examples information was made available to *estimate the profitability* of the advertising tested. For established brands, it was found that about 20% of advertising weight tests paid out (ie covered their costs) over the test year. The equivalent figure for new brands was higher, 40-50%[2].

6. *However, it was found in a number of cases that the sales increase above trend was maintained, at a diminishing rate, for a further year after the test had ended.* In one example which Abraham and Lodish quote[2], a 100% advertising weight increase in Year 1 produced sales increases above control of 7% in Year 1, 6% in Year 2 and 1% in Year 3. Over 15 case studies, the average sales increase was 22.4% in Year 1 (the test year), 17% in Year 2 and 6.2% in Year 3. In six of the 15 cases, the divergence between the samples actually widened in the year after the test ended[2]. *On average, when increased advertising has been successful in the first year, the cumulative incremental effect over the first year plus the following two years is twice that of the first year* (Lodish[79]). This is evidence that the immediate effect of an advertising burst, if the advertising is effective at all, continues to hold up in repeat purchasing after the burst ends at a rate which can take quite a long time to diminish back to its original level, and that the pattern varies considerably depending on the product. It also makes a substantial difference to the profitability calculations indicated in the last

paragraph.

7. IRI also run scanner based systems to estimate *the marginal profitability of promotions*, assessed against a projected baseline derived from unpromoted periods. *This was found to be even worse than advertising.* 'Only 16% of trade promotion events were profitable based upon their incremental sales of brands that are distributed through retailer warehouses. For many of the promotions, the cost of selling an incremental dollar of sales was *greater* than one dollar!' (Abraham and Lodish[1]). A major reason for this is 'forward buying': consumers, and retailers following them, stock up during the promotion and are able to postpone later purchases. Promotion effects are not found to continue over subsequent periods as advertising effects do.

8. It appears that *in-store displays and promotions inhibit the effect of increasing advertising weight.* The higher the level of display for an established brand, the less likely that the brand will show a sales increase following increased weight. The same applies to copy tests for established brands (Lubetkin[80]). No doubt what we see here is the instant sales response to instore promotion swamping the smaller movements that might be due to advertising.

9. However, there are also indications that *consumer promotions such as couponing, conversely, have a positive interaction with advertising*[80]. This again applies both to weight and copy tests, and suggests 'some synergies may exist between TV advertising and the advertising message which is communicated along with the coupon.'
The distinction between types of promotion that work with or against advertising may well correlate with what Prentice[92] has called 'consumer franchise building' activities, or

CFBs, and 'non-consumer franchise building' or Non-CFB activities. Examples of Non-CFBs are 'most of the manufacturer couponing being done today', as well as coupons in retailers' ads, price promotions and bonus packs, most premiums, sweepstakes, contests and refund offers, and all trade deals, allowances and advertising to the trade. Their functions are 'to accelerate the buying decision by temporarily reducing the price, by offering an extraneous incentive... or by getting retail distribution and trade featuring.' While essential, these Non-CFB activities do not by themselves 'register the brand's unique attributes in the consumer's mind.' CFBs, by contrast, include 'certain promotions which work like advertising', demonstrations and any service material that 'enhance perceptions of the unique value of a brand'. (Prentice[92])

All these findings are highly consistent with the common-sense theory we have been developing in the previous sections: only some advertising is effective; if it works it does so immediately *and* at the same time supports those brand values that maintain a permanent franchise; new brands show effects of growth whilst established brands are maintaining their place in an equilibrium and have much less scope to grow, if any. But there does not seem to be much that is new here (except perhaps the evidence on promotions). It looks like valuable supporting evidence, but only of things we already thought we knew. In particular, what are we to make of the high proportion of cases which do *not* show a visible sales increase on BehaviorScan? Abraham and Lodish argue that this is evidence of the waste in the system: advertisers should be more ready to discontinue campaigns or reduce their weight, depending on single-source tests for the supporting evidence, and should try even harder to find new campaign ideas to liven up their markets, replacing those which the tests show to be ineffective. Is this good advice?

The defensive role of advertising

On the contrary, I believe it could be very dangerous. The analysis so far described is not sensitive enough to show when an advertising campaign is in fact working well to hold the line for the brand, even though there is no immediate increment above trend in sales. Think again of the embattled stags. Suppose there was a market consisting of just two brands (to make it easy), which are competing for the same sector, and assume that both of them have very good advertising, which has pre-tested well, with an equivalent spend. Each on its own, without the other, would show an increment in a BehaviorScan test. But *what would happen to their sales if they were both fighting each other?* The market is mature: there is no room for overall sales to increase. In such a case, there is no scope to enlarge sales; but they could be lost to the other side, perhaps quite fast, if the pressure is allowed to slacken. There may well be such cases included in the 50% where we are led to think the advertising is not 'working', because no differential sales uplift can be seen.

We need some way of distinguishing between these cases and those where the advertising really is ineffective.

A better approach to analysing single-source data

There is a way, which has been known about for over twenty years, although for lack of attention the effort needed has never been put into developing it. This is to exploit the unique advantage of a single-source panel, which distinguishes it from any other data: the fact that it enables us to put together measures of purchasing behaviour, advertising exposure or opportunities to see, and other relevant variables attached to purchases (coupons, price reductions etc.) *within the same individuals over long periods of time.* This makes it possible to pose the key question, which can be generalised as follows: 'how does the behaviour of an individual person change after being exposed to advertising (etc), compared with when he has not been so exposed?'

The terms in this question can be varied for an infinity of situations: we have to define in each case the timing, 'exposure', behaviour, advertising, etc that we are talking about. Whether there are generalisable laws, or only specific ones for different types of product or stimulus, can only be determined after controlled exploration to build up examples. But the essential question is here: advertising is about causing change (or, just as important, preventing change which would otherwise happen) *within individuals*, so that they do something different afterwards. If, therefore, we look at people on our panel at this micro level over time, it should be possible (circling back to the question in the last section) to tell the difference between advertising which is working for the brand (even if for good reasons it cannot show a sales increase) and advertising which is not working at all.

Perhaps the major disappointment with the analysis of single-source panels which has been conducted so far, including what has been published from IRI, is that it has not progressed beyond the creation of test market comparisons between samples. Granted, the samples can now be matched much more accurately and relevantly than has ever been possible before; but, having been so matched, they are used no differently from traditional test market or AMTES data, or even from the way two samples would be compared from a mall intercept test. The question asked of the data is simply: does this test sample, which has been subjected to a different advertising treatment from the otherwise identical control sample, show a different value following that treatment in the dependent variable we are interested in, sales? There is nothing wrong with that approach as far as it goes; my complaint is that it adds nothing in kind, merely a slightly greater precision, to what has been done in the past before there was any possibility of single-source data. It is hardly surprising that it has merely repeated the same sorts of findings. Only by disaggregation is it possible to unlock the unique power of single-source panels to show us how *individuals* absorb, react and respond to stimuli.

People are different

Perhaps the most frequent sin in marketing is to assume that everybody in a group is the same. In fact, as Ehrenberg's models have shown, *most* people *most* of the time do not change their behaviour in response to advertising: they do not need to. Most advertisements are seen by people who are not interested in the subject at all, or who are not in a state to be persuaded any more than they already have been. But there are always a few who *will* respond in some way, *some* of the time. In most repeat purchase packaged goods markets, dramatic conversions from one brand to another are rare; most buyers have a repertoire of brands, some being bought more frequently than others. Most of the time, most buyers have no incentive to change these habits; but sometimes a few may fail to repeat their regular purchase and replace with a second rank or even a new brand. There may be all sorts of reasons for wanting a change, perhaps no more than simple enjoyment of variety. Sometimes the change will coincide with a promotion or a new advertisement that catches attention, or a drop in advertising for the old brand. Perhaps seeing the new brand calls up an advertising memory which has lodged at the back of the mind. There are probably a few consumers who are particularly changeable and prone to follow advertising or promotion changes. The value of studying disaggregated single-source data is that then, and only then, could one hope to learn in detail how to understand these patterns; who responds, under what circumstances. And, if there are effects at the detailed level which do not show up in overall increases in sales, but are working to maintain the brand, we should be able to see them.

Previous experience with 'within person' analysis

The key to the analysis we want is that it is 'within person': are the same people more likely to buy when they have been exposed to advertising than when they have not? In posing this question to the data, one has to take care, as in all analysis, to ensure that the observed effects can safely be attributed to the advertising and not some other variable. More than twenty years ago, some results were reported from a small experimental single-source panel run by J Walter Thompson in London, long before the technological advances described above were available (McDonald[83]). Data came from paper diaries kept by 250 housewives in the London area for 13 weeks, giving day by day purchasing, TV viewing and magazine and newspaper readership. Nine product fields were analysed. The objective set up was to see from the brand switching patterns whether housewives were more likely to switch *to* a brand, or less likely to switch *away from* it, when they had received more advertising (defined as 'opportunities to see' or OTS, because they had looked at the commercial break or the magazine issue containing advertising for that brand) during the interval since their last purchase.

The hypothesis that OTS would affect switching patterns was confirmed for each product field, although not necessarily for each brand within a field (the sample being too small for this). Equally important, it was done in such a way that one could be confident that a real effect was being observed, not a spurious relationship. The key results were as follows.

1. Purchasers were more likely both to *switch to* a brand and to *stay with* it if they had received advertising (defined throughout as OTS) in the purchasing interval (the space of time elapsed since the previous purchase). This was evidence that advertising can both attract and reinforce.

2. The incremental effects were strongest when there had been *one or two* OTS, and tailed off for three, four or more. In other words, the added effects of increasing frequency of potential exposure were not limitless, adding fuel to the question of how to define the 'right' level of frequency, above which extra weight is wasted.

3. If *only switches* were looked at, the same effect was found: a larger proportion of switches *into or out of* a brand were *into* the brand when there had been more OTS for that brand in the previous interval, and again the effect levelled off above two OTS. This was the clinching evidence that we were not looking at a spurious relationship, because of the fact that, within each individual purchasing sequence, the number of switches into and out of any brand are equal, plus or minus one (depending on where the sequence is cut). This means that, if advertising has no effect, we would expect the ratio of in/out switches to be 50/50, whatever the OTS, and the results are by definition independent of variables related to *people*, such as where they shop, their media consumption, etc. It is a true 'within person' measurement.

4. The effects were even stronger when OTS were looked at within four days before the purchase, thus cutting out advertising seen at the start of a long interval, which might be supposed to have a diminishing effect. This was evidence of advertising, when it works, working immediately. There has been other evidence since supporting the view that advertising can have a quick reminding/triggering effect which diminishes rapidly as days pass.

5. There was evidence of the effects showing in share of voice terms: advertising can be more effective when it is outweighing the competition. This is important for investigating the

question posed above: how to distinguish between advertising which is not working at all and advertising which *is* working, but in equilibrium with other brands.

There has been sadly little experimental follow-up of this early study, at least published, although what there is has tended to confirm the main findings[41, 32, 19]. It is a very limited analysis, as far as it goes. The few examples visible of advertising being followed by a behaviour shift at the next purchase can only be a tip of a very much larger iceberg: we need to extend the analysis to explain purchasing patterns as a whole. Also, as Broadbent[19] has pointed out, there are other variables, especially price and promotions, which may have their own immediate effect, and which may interact with advertising. These interactions need to be understood. The IRI study has suggested their existence, but we need to understand the mechanism; for example, if a promotion adds to purchases of a brand or merely brings them forward in time, and if this is more likely in the presence of advertising, longitudinal analysis of individual patterns should enable us to *see* it.

Analysis of buying patterns

One interesting paper (McQueen[84]) gives a foretaste of what could be possible if single-source data are analysed properly. Leo Burnett in Chicago used IRI data (not the data set in the 'Advertising Works' study, but an experimental set from IRI's Eau Claire market released for academic purposes some years ago) to discover how brand growth relates to buying habits. Five types of buying pattern were identified:

- loyals, who are 'involved with the brand',

- rotators, who move between brands but are 'involved with the category',

- deal selectives, who always tend to buy on a promotion,

- price driven, exceptionally sensitive to price,

- light users, who buy the category so seldom that one cannot detect a strategy.

51 growing brands were modelled, and it was found that, for different brands, different segments accounted for the growth by increasing their buying rate. Maxwell House, for example, grew 69% in the area during the year studied: the rate of buying grew 56%, mostly accounted for by the 'rotators' (46% growth); new users of the brand grew by 27%, balanced by 13% who lapsed, so that the net penetration growth was 14%. Another growing brand, Del Monte Ketchup, grew 25% over-all, with 16% gain in buying rate and 10% net penetration growth; but here the main buying rate gains were among the 'deal selectives', who accounted for 12% of the 16% growth in the rate. A third brand, Hunts Ketchup, grew mainly among 'loyals'.

These examples were given in the paper quoted to show that brands grow by existing users increasing their rate of buying rather than by penetration growth, and that single-source data can help to identify the right target in terms of buying habits. It is tantalising to think how much farther this could be taken if one could put these buyer segments together with their oppor-tunities to see advertising, traced individually over time. Incidentally, the finding that growth is buying-rate led, not penetration led, is perfectly consistent with the Ehrenberg result that brands differ in penetration rather than in purchase fre-quency. Existing users are the holders of the brands equity; if it increases permanently (taking from competition), new users are sucked in at the bottom end and the old equilibrium re-establishes itself at a new level (see argument on pp 37-38). Such growth, of course, may easily not be permanent, when the campaign is over and the competition has gathered itself together. It would be interesting to know, for instance, how lasting a growth dependent on 'rotators' will be.

Scope for single-source analyses

With the databases now available, the scope for such analyses is very large. It should be possible to pull out data on buyers grouped according to the behaviour patterns identified by Ehrenberg's models: frequent buyers of Brand A who also buy Brand B, infrequent buyers of A who also buy B, etc. We then need to study how these distinctive groups of buyers respond to all the different variables and their combinations. We will expect to find that *some* brand advertising evokes a response which we can see immediately, but not all; that it may vary with frequency and, more importantly, with *timing* and *share of voice*; that it may sometimes, but not always, interact with other marketing variables such as promotions or price. The form of question is always, with many variations on the basic theme: how does this group of consumers behave differently when they have seen advertising compared with when they have not?

If this type of analysis were routinely done, the good news is that it would become much less urgent to set up difficult and costly test market experiments; the controls are applied within respondents, not between samples. If an advertisement 'works', it should be possible to see it working at the micro level, even if the aggregate test results do not show a clear-cut sales gain. The problem is that, to look at the important sub-groups, one would need a reasonably large sample over a long enough time. But it is recommended that test markets should be conducted for at least a year, if not longer, and in that time it would be possible to ensure enough exposure.

Summary: effects on sales

1. *Perceptions of how advertising affects sales*, and how these effects can be measured, crucially affect the value which manufacturers place on advertising; therefore, they cannot be avoided in a discussion of how advertising may work.

2. *Advertising works both immediately and in the long-term.* The distinction has long been recognised, but has been the cause of some muddled thinking. The problem has arisen largely because most sales measures have been inevitably short-term, which has led some to question the value of taking account of long-term effects in setting budgets: if short-term volume and market share increases are seen as the only measurable marketing goal, theme advertising is often not the most cost-effective way of achieving these, and in-store and other promotions may seem more attractive (if one is prepared to ignore the revenue cost). It is suggested that it would be advisable to stop regarding long- and short-term effects as different, and to see them instead as part of the same continuum: each effective advertising stimulus now adds to the deposit of what previous brand-building has achieved (alternatively, provides the continuing energy supply needed by the brand in its struggle against competition).

3. *Econometric* and similar methods are discussed. They are used to clarify hypotheses about the reasons why sales move, and as instruments for trying out 'what if?' scenarios. Their limitations are mainly connected with their being dependent on short-term variations in sales and their consequent difficulty in dealing with the long-term effects of advertising (or, to put it another way, the 'base' which a brand has reached as opposed to increments upon it). It is noted that 'sales' throughout means (or should mean, if people are thinking properly) 'effective sales' related to price: a price increase

which sells the same amount is as valuable as a price reduction which sells more, and therefore we should be looking at the 'demand curve' of price against quantity and the price elasticities. The *adstock* calculation can help take account of decaying effects of advertising in an econometric model.

A less noticed limitation of econometrics is the apparent assumption that sales are to be explained by independent and additive variables such as advertising expenditure measures, promotions and so on, whereas in real life these are likely to be interactive and multiplicative: either they all work for an individual or none do. Underlying this again appears to be an old-fashioned notion of cause and effect.

4. The importance of *maintaining the base* is discussed, and the danger that can arise if this is neglected ('Death of a brand'). Short-term changes are fluctuations around this base, or 'brand equity', level. Modellers have difficulty dealing with sales increments and 'the base', seen as separate components, and the same data can produce contradictory findings according to how the definition is made. Broadbent proposes an elegant and surely better approach, in which the base/increment distinction is abolished and sales are seen as a combination of price effects, distribution effects and 'brand equity', the result of other short- or long-term influences, including advertising. This parallels the proposal to abolish the distinction between advertising short- and long-term effects.

5. The other way of measuring effects on sales is via *single-source data*, in which purchasing and opportunities for advertising exposure are collected from a panel of individuals over time. The technology to make this possible has been developed in the United States through IRI's test market

facilities, and national services from IRI/Arbitron and Nielsen are now becoming available. IRI's review of nearly 400 tests, now issued under the title 'How Advertising Works', produced some equivocal-seeming results: success may, but does not necessarily, follow weight or copy test scores; it is easier to see effects with new brands or treatments than with established brands. There is some welcome evidence about the long-term effect of advertising continuing to show on sales some time after the advertising has stopped.

6. *A weakness* of the testing system as reported is that it relies on aggregate comparisons between matched samples, of which is exposed to the greater weight or new copy, etc; it has not exploited the key advantage of a single-source panel reporting continuously, that relationships between advertising and purchasing can be examined *within individuals over time.* It is argued that this level of analysis is now necessary if we are to progress in learning exactly how advertising produces responses in people with different relevant purchasing habits, and how this varies with different concentrations and competitive activity, interacts with promotions, etc. McDonald's[83] analysis of over twenty years ago on a JWT experimental panel shows what methods and discoveries are possible.

Within person analysis is the key to being able to distinguish between advertising which is working effectively to defend a brand's position, but does not show up in a sales or share increase against strong competition in a stable market, and advertising which is not working at all.

5 Response to advertising: effects on the mind

We have seen that it is sometimes possible to observe effects on sales that we can attribute to advertising, although the conditions in which we can do so are limited. But we cannot stop short at behavioural responses, important though these are, for two obvious reasons. First, short-term sales measures, including those from single-source panels, can only apply to frequently purchased products; but increasing amounts of advertising are devoted to occasional, considered purchases, or to aims which are not purchases at all but beliefs and opinions. For these, we have no choice but to look at how people respond in thoughts and feelings, rather than actions. Secondly, merely knowing that sales have responded may be good for accountability but is of little prescriptive use; we have to understand *how* effects are achieved if we want to improve what we are doing. That includes understanding of whatever may be going on even when we cannot observe an adequate short term sales effect, since, as we have seen, this is rarely a sufficient ground for valuing advertising: 'we get excited when we find identifiable sales effects; but the plain fact is that they are usually far too small to pay for the advertising for established brands' (Brown[20]).

We now turn, therefore, to the *psychological* aspect of advertising response: what goes on in people's heads, and how this may relate to what they do. 'Immediacy characterises all effective advertising' (Jones[58]), but how?

No simple single solution
The frustration (and the fascination, since one cannot leave it alone) of the advertising effectiveness question is that it is so elusive. The literature often seems to read like an elephants' graveyard of discarded theories (AIDA, the USP, etc). These theories have often seemed intuitively powerful (Joyce[64]), but

partial: they are helpful ways of looking at *some* aspects of *some* advertising, but are quickly falsified as total explanations as soon as we find examples that do not fit.

Few thoughtful practitioners now believe that there can be a simple account of how 'advertising' works. It depends on the context and purpose: new brands, new formulations of established brands, frequent and trivial or rare and considered purchases, type of behaviour or attitudes wanted, etc. It is natural now to sympathise with Stephen King: 'What we need … is not a wholly comprehensive theory of advertising, but a slightly more advanced *theory of advertisements*. A framework for thinking how different sorts of advertisement might work, for different people, in different circumstances, at different stages of time. With such complexity, the framework should be simple enough to be of practical use to the people who have the job of planning and creating advertisements, and those who have the job of evaluating them.' (King[67]).

How advertisers and agency planners think it works

Perhaps, however, one is premature in thinking that such sensible ideas are now normal. Hall and Maclay[43] report an interesting study amongst agency account directors and planners and advertisers' marketing and research staffs. They were asked to agree or disagree with a wide range of statements about 'how advertising works', which were factor analysed; the respondents were then clustered on the main factors. One has, perhaps, to be cautious about findings generated by a research technique based on belief statements which informants may well have found difficulty responding to in such a complex conceptual area; however, the statements used were based on depth interviews among the same group of people, and the main hypotheses to be quantified were identified at this stage. The authors concluded that there were five main conceptual 'models', which they named as follows:

- *The Sales Response model.* Sales is the only indicator of campaign effectiveness. Intermediate measures have no reliable predictive value.

- *The Persuasion model.* Advertising works, and can be measured, through a linear sequence from awareness to understanding to choice.

- *The Involvement model.* The purpose of advertising is to 'build a relationship with consumers by talking to them intelligently and entertainingly'.

- *The Salience model.* Advertising differentiates the product, makes it stand out.

- *The Commodity model.* Really a non-model, mostly held by small advertisers and non-users of agencies; advertising is entirely functional.

The point of interest here is that the sample studied tended to adhere, temperamentally or because of their company cultures, to one or other of these models, and this could have profound effects on the ways they evaluate advertising, set budgets and use research. Only the middle three contain theories about how advertising may work: as such, they are 'representative of three different orientations very much prevalent within the advertising industry' (Prue[93]). The Sales model, which we have already argued is incomplete because it would judge advertising solely by the stimulation of short-term sales movements, was subscribed to by 'a distinct cluster of advertisers who...accounted for 19% of our quantitative sample[43].

This recent example makes clear that the sophistication shown nowadays by serious writers on advertising, and their openness to the idea that it may have different tasks depending on the context, is not necessarily shared by those who operate it. The simple theory still has strong intuitive ('common-sense, gut-feel') power, and can be hard to shake, unless one can produce clear empirical evidence; even then, it can be ignored.

Two basic views of advertising
Sequential models and necessary conditions

The Persuasion model referred to above implies a sequence of stages, in which the task of advertising is first to communicate something; secondly, when they are aware of it they can be persuaded to like it; finally, once convinced, they are moved to act accordingly. This way of thinking has been so extensively criticised that it is a surprise to find it still evidently alive and well, being endorsed by 38% of the Hall/Maclay sample. We need to understand why it is apparently so appealing, as well as its limitations.

The idea of the sequence has taken a number of forms:

- *Starch* (1925[101]): an advertisement must be seen – read – believed – remembered – *acted upon.*

- *DAGMAR* (Colley, 1961[23]): perhaps the best known version. An advertisement must carry the prospective customer through four levels of understanding: awareness – comprehension – conviction – action.

- *AIDA*: attention – interest – desire – action.

- *AIETA*: awareness – interest – evaluation – trial – adoption.

Such models have been generally christened 'hierarchy of

effects' or 'linear sequential' models. It has been noted of them that they are intuitive and true by tautology (Joyce[64]). In other words, they could be called 'necessary condition' models. We must be aware of something in order to want it, and we must want it in order to buy it, but this does not work the other way round: we can be aware and not want, etc. This logic explains much of the instinctive appeal of these approaches. It also led to an important practical consequence: it legitimised the measurement of 'intermediate' variables such as awareness and image as surrogates for sales. The argument was that sales (at least before econometrics) were too far removed and contaminated with other variables to be reliable measures of effect, whereas awareness, for example, is directly related to advertising and responsive to it in a way we can more easily see; if awareness is a necessary condition for sales, it becomes a good excuse for abandoning the latter with relief.

The other point about these models is that there are *some* advertising contexts for which they are at least reasonable. When people are thinking about a new product which they have not used before, or a serious purchase such as a new car or an insurance policy, they might well go through the mental processes described, perhaps in quite an elaborate way. 'They imply a rational consumer weighing up the arguments – the object of advertising is seen as being to present persuasive arguments.'[64].

There is also the whole area of *direct response* advertising: direct mail, or print advertising which is aimed at getting people to clip a coupon. It has become easy to overlook direct response when thinking is dominated by television, but the attitudes formed in the days of Claude Hopkins, with his insistence that advertising can and must always be tested by results (*Scientific Advertising*, written in 1923[47]) can be seen clearly in the background of hierarchy of effects theories. Advertising which elicits a direct response *does* presuppose that people first see it, grasp what is on offer and then make a decision. What more natural, for those brought up with such expectations, than to seek to apply them to the new situation in which there are no direct responses to show that something has been 'learnt'.

The criticism, which is extensive in the literature, is based on two main arguments. The first is that very many, probably most, purchasing situations simply do not involve this stylised rational decision making; especially, it does not apply to things which are bought repetitively out of habit. There is empirical evidence to show that the sequential logic breaks down: attitudes follow behaviour rather than preceding it; people try things out and *then* decide whether they like them; people are affected by emotions and moods at least as much as reason. The second is that the sequential model seems to imply a passive consumer, who is moved from one stage of thinking to the next in a uniform way: 'a *tabula rasa* on which messages are printed' (Lannon and Cooper[76]).

The myth of the passive consumer

I am not convinced that this last objection is quite fair: the picture of the 'rational consumer weighing up the arguments' does not necessarily imply passivity, especially if we see the 'stages' in the sequence as *necessary conditions* rather than automatic causes. But it is undeniable that thinking about advertising has suffered in the past from what might be termed 'the myth of the passive consumer'. This attitude of mind is buried deep in traditional language about advertising, when people talk of making an *impact* (like a steel ball striking a wall), or people receiving *impressions* (like wax), or messages being *hammered home* (like nails). These are all unconscious metaphors of advertising *doing things to* people. It is closely related to the desire for simple causal inferences which we noted when discussing short-term sales effects: we desperately want to be able to say what *causes* sales, and slip naturally from that into asking what 'causes' people to act or take a decision.

Even if we dislike this causal mythology, it is worth the effort to appreciate why it has been so seductive. The attraction of the physical cause-and-effect model is that it enables one to consider attaching equal values to the 'units' of advertising (exposures, OTS or TVRs). If each unit has its own little 'electric charge' which it transmits to whatever is moved, we ought to be able to find out what the formula is, calculate what effect each of the parts contributes to the whole, and then try the effect of different weights, etc. (see argument in McDonald[82]).

Another implicit reason for the long persistence of the 'passive consumer' is that it suggests uniformity – people or groups all responding the same way to a stimulus – and uniformity is a *simplifying* factor. The picture of a whole population understanding and accepting one's message in essentially the same way is easy to grasp, and therefore attractive. To suggest that, in reality, there is a huge diversity of ways in which people will understand or fail to understand what one is trying to say can be confusing and unsettling.

A third and more sinister reason has been well noted by Jeremy Bullmore[21]. If consumers are passive, it is a short step to seeing them as *manipulable*, and thus excellent ammunition for the generation brought up on Vance Packard's *Hidden Persuaders*. 'Television advertising', says Bullmore, 'began to have an extremely adverse effect on the reputation of advertising as a trade – at any rate among the chattering classes. Television advertising possessed two characteristics which the middle classes found intolerable. First, it was intrusive – which is to say that it was noticed. And, secondly, it worked. Here was clear evidence that vulnerable and sophisticated people – in other words, the sort of people who would watch television – were being manipulated, almost certainly subliminally, by sociology graduates who had been brainwashed by capitalism.' Those who wish to take a political position opposed to advertising undoubtedly find it helpful to their argument if they can portray consumers as 'passive'.

If the relationship between advertising OTS and sales was obviously indirect, causal chains were manufactured to link each 'element' of mental process to the next. Even if DAGMAR and the rest do not have to be read this way, there is not much doubt that it was how they were often seen. It is largely because of their implication that the recipients of advertising are 'passive' units that these so-called 'transmission models' have been so comprehensively attacked in recent years, by those who are actually involved in the advertising process.

The active consumer: what people do with advertising

The alternative view states that, so far from responding passively, those who receive advertising are *actively in control, and pick and choose what they will attend to*. This way of seeing things has very largely displaced the other, at least among those who have anything directly to do with advertising. It has many attractive implications.

- *It fits what we know about purchasing behaviour* on a much wider scale, including low-involvement, habitual purchasing where there is no sense in 'a sequence of causal steps'.

- So far from each advertisement carrying its own 'energy charge', it has no value at all *unless the recipient chooses to give it one*. Otherwise, it is simply screened out. 'We talk of impacts, as if the advertising message was the dominant element, making its mark on a passive individual. The reality is very different, with the considerations which an individual brings to any contact with an advertisement playing the dominant role.' (Smith[99])

- Following this, one may note that *most advertisements are of no interest to most people, most of the time.* Winston Fletcher has recently written: 'I am not the least bit interested in buying most of the things I see advertised. Indeed I won't buy them. Nor will you. Nobody is influenced by most of the advertisements they see. A few individual advertisements benefit each of us, in innumerable ways, every day of the week; but the great majority of advertisements are irrelevant to us.' (Fletcher[37])

- *To sort out the few advertisements of interest to them, people use their power of selective perception.* Fletcher draws a distinction between *intrusive* and *non-intrusive* advertisements. Non-intrusive advertising, perhaps 40-50% of the total, is advertising which people will actively seek or scan when they have a need or an interest, but will ignore at other times: examples are most classified advertising, eg for homes or jobs, holidays or theatres, financial offers, much 'price and line' advertising (which assumes that customers are looking for a particular make at the cheapest price), hobby advertising, and some business-to-business advertising in trade and technical publications. This kind of advertising simply has to be there; interested customers know where to seek it out, 'look for it of their own volition', or register it if they see it accidentally.

- *Intrusive advertising, on the other hand, is for things you would not go searching for*: they are low-involvement, low-interest, and you are not in a buying mood. Automatically, to avoid being overwhelmed, the mind screens them out. To get through this screen and be noticed, advertisements must 'intrude' in the sense that there is something about them to attract attention. Fletcher suggests that there are four ways in which advertisements do this, by analogy with spotting faces in a crowd.

When you walk down a crowded street, you see hundreds of people. Almost all of them pass unnoticed, but a tiny handful make some impact on you. You notice them and perhaps remember their faces afterwards. You may notice and remember them because:

— they are unusual, they 'stand out', because they are physically different (eg beautiful or ugly, very tall or very short, etc);

— they 'stand out' because they have made themselves *seem* different (eg in dress or behaviour);

— something about them has relevance for *you personally* (eg you are interested in what they are wearing, or they remind you of someone you know);

— a face in the crowd is actually a face you were looking for, or is already familiar to you (an old friend).

In the same way, advertisements 'stand out' if:

— the product advertised is different or special;

— it is advertised in an unusual or striking way;

— the advertisement is particularly, personally relevant to you;

— it is an advertisement you have got to know well.

The best advertising will often work in all four of these ways.[37]

- *Nobody can be forced to buy a product he does not want, or to change his beliefs and opinions against his will, or to pay attention to advertising which is not of interest to him.* This puts a premium on the need to *target* advertising, with targets defined not so much in terms of characteristics (eg demographic or psychographic types, although these can have some relevance) as of interests or moods. The advertiser will be most effective if he can find the 'right way to speak to' those who are prone to be interested in what he has to say.

  Gordon Brown, also writing recently, quotes evidence from the Millward Brown tracking experience with low-involvement, frequently purchased products that the chief difference in attitudes is between users and non-users of a brand[20]. Most will recognise this as true from their own experience of tracking surveys. It confirms not only that positive attitudes accompany and are reinforced by successful brand experience, rather than preceding it, but also that *current users* are the appropriate target for established brand advertising – not only because they account for most sales (especially the more frequent users) but also because any new users who are likely to be attracted can be expected to be *like* the users, to share their interests (this, from a different angle, supports the buying pattern evidence from IRI quoted above (McQueen[84]).

- Brown also stresses *the importance of people being in the right mood for receiving advertising.* When they say in answers to survey questions that they are 'not persuaded by' advertising, they are telling the truth. When they are watching TV (or being asked questions), that is precisely the time when they 'are *not* disposed to reconsider their shopping habits'. They are defensive of their habits, and resistant to 'advertising' recognised as such. It is when they are actually in the purchasing situation, deciding what to pick off the shelf, that *perhaps* something relevant in the advertising they have seen may be remembered; a fleeting interest previously aroused may recur to reinforce the thought that 'perhaps I'll try this today'. (Brown[20]).

- Finally, if people respond to advertising in this selective way, *it follows that they also respond to other influences, such as price or promotions, in a similar way.* This reinforces the view that it is unhelpful to regard them as independent variables each with its own 'value'; on the contrary, we must expect them to reinforce each other when the marketing programme is working well.

Which view is most appealing?
The person-centred view is fruitful, credible and attractive. For most practitioners these days, the vision of 'people doing things with advertising' has displaced, in most contexts, the vision of 'advertising doing things to people'. To sum it up, it is irresistible to quote Jeremy Bullmore again:

'The critics of advertising know that consumers can be *made* to consume in ever increasing quantities. Advertisers *want* consumers to consume in ever increasing quantities. Agencies do their best to *persuade* consumers to consume in ever increasing quantities. And yet, only too often, they don't.
The blame, then, lies inescapably at the feet of the consumer. I'm afraid it has to be said: the consumer of

today is quite frequently guilty of gross irresponsibility. "look here," I sometimes feel like saying to them, "you're a consumer, aren't you? Then why the hell aren't you out there consuming?"[21]

Note, however, that both positions are essentially *intuitive*: they cannot be scientifically proved. They are working hypotheses which we adopt to the extent that they enable us to make sense of the facts as we know them and provide the best framework for fertile and productive ideas. Note also that someone who leans towards either view can use the same specific ideas and evidence to support his position. For example, DAGMAR and similar sequential models can still be fitted in by those who believe that 'people do things with advertising', especially if we see the stages in the models as necessary conditions (you can't buy something if you don't know about it) rather than causal stimuli (you've got to know about it first).

In other words, these two alternative mind-sets are not really models of how advertising works: they are at a stage farther back than that. We interpret the specific models against the background they provide. In the same way, an evolutionist will interpret what is known about genetic inheritance and the fossil record against the background of his basic belief in evolution, whereas a fundamentalist will set the same facts against his quite different interpretative preferences. Karl Popper has called such working hypotheses, like evolution theory, 'metaphysical research programmes', because, while themselves beyond proof, they provide a fruitful basis for thinking and help us to make sense of the world[91]. In the same way, those who have adopted the person-centred view of advertising ('people do things with it') have done so because, ultimately, they feel more comfortable with it and it explains more for them.

As with the theory of evolution, the 'active consumer' theory, with its acceptance of diversity and choice, has steadily gained ground over recent years. However, the 'passive consumer' is still alive and well in certain quarters, and surfaces every now and again in the tone used to talk about advertising. This very day, as I write, the Newspaper Publishers Association has placed an advertisement attacking television advertising on the ground that two-thirds of TV advertising expenditure is 'wasted' because it has been shown that, two-thirds of the time, people leave the room when commercials are on, or zap to other channels, or simply do not pay attention (the argument is based on an experiment by Dr Peter Collett, who filmed people while watching television using a camera hidden in the TV set). The flavour of this copy is pure 'passive consumer': two-thirds of the commercials are not watched, therefore two-thirds are wasted. The implication is clear: if watched, it will not be wasted, it will move people. They go on to use the following language: 'Newspaper advertisements can be intrusive, powerful and compelling' – all 'passive consumer' words.

Long-term memory and short-term responses

In discussing effects on sales, we saw that advertising, if it works at all, has both an immediate effect and a 'continuing' effect: 'this is another way of saying that it builds added values, which ... operate in conjunction with consumer satisfaction with a brand's functional properties to ensure repeat purchase of the brand in a competitive marketplace.' (Jones[58]). We now have a mechanism explaining how this can happen. If an advertisement is interesting for some reason, it may come back to mind later, when consumers are thinking about the brand (Brown[20]). Similarly, it can happen the other way round: memory of the brand, and the experience of using it, may be brought to mind when they see the advertising. This long-term memory is not automatic, but is set off 'via associations, linkages and triggers'. For established brands, a major function of continuous advertising is to keep reinforcing this long-term memory, so that it continues to be easily triggered.

What exactly is lodged in the memory may vary. It may be the advertisement itself: but here, if what is remembered has no involvement with the brand, it may well be an ineffective trigger, however exciting or amusing. It may be the brand, or something in the advertisement related to the brand. The advertisement may have contributed to lodging the brand in the memory without any trace of itself remaining, in which case the advertisement would have affected the brand memory at the point of purchase without the brand actually reminding of the advertisement. The possibilities are hugely variable and complex.

Several points fall into place with this account. We can see how advertising not only creates immediate interest but at the same time interacts with all the previous images (and experiences) of the brand; it builds on the past and carries forward into the future. It explains how advertising which keeps ringing changes on a proven successful theme can keep a brand going indefinitely, as in the case of the PG Tips chimps: the memory triggers work because they are familiar and loved, and the changes are just enough to keep the idea vivid and alive.

It is also consistent with the observation of short-term sales or purchasing effects we have noted from within-person analysis of single-source data. Some people, some of the time, are sensitive to advertising memory triggers, and more so if the memory is relatively fresh. In a very few, tip-of-iceberg cases, we can see such triggers playing a part at the point where the purchase is made.

The concept of 'long-term memory' is also the only way one can really make sense of the *advertising awareness* measure of effectiveness, which is the stock in trade of the Millward Brown measurement (the Advertising Index). There are considerable problems in practice with the concept of 'advertising awareness' and how it may be disentangled from awareness of the brand: but let us assume that what is measured is genuinely a recollection of advertising seen. The form of question used by Millward Brown is to ask whether, and what, advertising has been seen for a named brand recently: in other words, the brand is used as the trigger for the advertising memory, as if it were a surrogate purchasing occasion. In that sense, movements in the awareness index can be seen as evidence of fluctuating strength or weakness in the *long-term memory*. It does not, of course, on its own tell one whether that memory is relevant to one's objective. We all remember advertising for things we do not buy, and vice versa.

Summary: response to advertising - effects on the mind

1. Sales measures can only apply to a limited selection of products and services, and they do not go far in telling us how people respond to advertising. We have to consider the *psychological* aspect: the effect on the mind.

2. Few now believe that any single theory can explain how advertising can lead to behaviour change. The Hall and Maclay study quoted[43] shows evidence, however, that *advertising practitioners tend to work to a single intuitive, 'common-sense' model of the process*, and identified five such, including: sales are the only relevant criteria; advertising 'persuades' by moving people from awareness to action; advertising is for building a relationship with consumers and 'involving' them; advertising is for differentiating the brand. These cultural preferences may largely determine how different people approach advertising.

3. Underlying these concepts of persuasion, involvement etc are two possible mental orientations: one is to see consumers as essentially *passive*, and moved by advertising; the other is to see them as the *active* party, engaged in making choices

and deciding whether or not to pay attention to advertising. Both of these are intuitive ways of interpreting the world and, as such, are not susceptible of proof; any facts can be fitted into either scheme. We adopt whichever view we feel most comfortable with. But over the past few years there has been a substantial shift from the 'passive consumer' to the 'active consumer' view.

4. The 'passive consumer' underlies the *sequential models* which represent advertisements as shifting people along a mental continuum from awareness to conviction to behaviour. Such models are most easily understood if expressed as *necessary conditions*: one must be aware before one can believe, etc. They have been generally abandoned as explanations of advertising in general, because many, probably most, situations do not conform to the sequential logic. They are an appropriate way of thinking in those cases where purchases genuinely involve serious, rational decisions, and in the area of direct response advertising.

5. The 'active consumer' recognises that most people, most of the time, have no interest in the advertisements they see, that selective perception operates, and that what is not wanted is screened out. It has become more acceptable as the advertising clutter has grown, and with it the perceived need to target advertising ever more carefully so that it will speak to those most likely to find it relevant and interesting, especially the existing product users or those who are like them. It also recognises the importance of emotional elements in consumer response.

6. The hypothesis is discussed that advertising may involve the *long-term memory*, so that its effect is delayed-action, triggered at the time when, for example, a shopper is faced with

the brand as she is about to make a purchase. Such long-term memory seems to be the best way of making sense of 'advertising awareness', assuming that this concept is accurately measurable, and it is consistent with the idea of the advertising continuum proposed above, in which the memory of a well-loved theme can be continually refreshed by advertising which reverts to it in an interesting way. The ways in which advertising or brands are remembered, and the relevance of such memories to purchasing habits, can obviously vary greatly, and the task for much advertising for established brands can be seen as making sure that the memory triggers are useful.

6 What kinds of response are possible?

We now have a framework in which we can discuss advertising as an instrument which:

— elicits (or, more properly perhaps, invites) response,
— in so doing, sustains and builds the product (branding),
— works in with other influences on the same side (deals, pricing),
— is modified by competitive influences, including other brands' advertising,
— can be shown to result, when successful, in sustaining sales and market share (when a brand has reached its equilibrium in a stable market) or developing them (where there is still capacity to grow).

But *how* do we do these things? *What* responses succeed, and how do we achieve them? What *sort* of thing works best?

Variety, and the place for old saws

It is at this point that one starts to read the manuals and words of wisdom written by advertising men. One of the first things they tend to tell you is about the huge variety of purposes which advertising can have, and therefore of responses it can seek. This is an easy point to grasp: one has only to think of the differences between advertising, say, baked beans, perfume, cars, ICI, a building society savings account, a new law about passengers wearing rear seatbelts.

It would be possible to take refuge in this diversity and argue, as many have been tempted to do, that advertising is so varied that it makes any kind of generalisation impossible; every single advertisement is unique, and to look for guiding principles is chasing after fools' gold. To quote Winston Fletcher again: 'The quest for a formula which will guarantee successful advertising is as futile as the quest for the Holy Grail ... Consumers react to advertisements in an infinite variety of ways, and each new advertisement generates subtly different responses from its innumerable predecessors.' And again: 'To attempt to squeeze potato crisp, patent medecine and political advertising into the same mould as each other is as futile as it would be to enter a St Bernard in the Greyhound Derby or to send a chihuahua padding through the snows toting a brandy barrel round its tiny neck.'[37]

If we take this view to its extreme, even the words of the wise old men (the David Ogilvies and James Webb Youngs) become irrelevant: creativity is all, and every new advertisement is a fresh creative act, no more and no less. But it is hard to feel comfortable with this extreme view. St Bernards, greyhounds and chihuahuas are very different, but they are still all dogs. We cannot help feeling that there must be some features, or constraints, which apply peculiarly to advertisements, for all their creative variety.

And indeed we find that, having acknowledged the variety, many commentators are able to find some unifying principles. The following are two well-known examples; it is well beyond the scope of this book to cover them all, even of those that have been published, and I hope I will be forgiven by other disciples for omitting their particular guru.

Two well-known schemes
The scale of responses

One way of categorising responses which may be sought from consumers is in terms of how close they are to direct action. This approach has been associated for some years with J Walter Thompson in London; Jones[58] has christened it the 'King Continuum', after Stephen King, who invented it.

From the point of view of the consumer, desired responses can be classified along a scale ranging from 'direct' to 'indirect'. The scale runs as follows.

Direct   1. *Take action.* This advertising aims 'to get people to pull out a pen, fill in the coupon, sign a cheque, address an envelope and mail it, or call a number'. The response sought is 'I'll do that or buy that now'.

          This would typically be for infrequent, low involvement products for which there are not very clear-cut branded markets, where the task is to overcome inertia or indifference.

    2. *Seek information.* The response here is 'That sounds interesting; I'll find out more about it'. There is an immediate response, asking for information, but it is the new information that leads to choice.

          This tends to be for infrequently purchased goods, especially if they are complex or expensive, so that the decision requires thought and the comparison of alternatives: for instance, durables, holidays, cars, insurance, savings. The advertising helps to get the brand onto the list of brands for the buyer to consider.

    3. *Relate to needs, wants, desires.* The advertising aims to get people to make the link between the brand and their needs or desires. Although an immediate effect is aimed at, there is no immediate action. Buying takes place on the next suitable occasion, when long-term memory of the advertising may be activated by seeing the brand or some other display in the store. The response is something like: 'This is just the thing for me'.

          This advertising is particularly aimed at trial of a new brand, or of something which is only occasionally used, such as proprietary drugs, or cosmetics/toiletries which constantly appear in new varieties. It works largely by presenting 'news'.

4. *Bring to top of mind, recall previous satisfactions.* The response here is 'That reminds me'. This is advertising for repeat purchase, habit dominated products for which people develop a repertoire of brands they find acceptable. The advertising keeps the brand at the top of the short list, and reorders the list when it has slipped. The Hall and Maclay 'Salience model' fits here. The advertising stops the brand being forgotten.

5. *Modify attitudes.* This is advertising which seeks to change perceptions and attitudes towards a brand, which may take months or even years. The intended response is 'I never thought of it like that before'. This advertising role becomes appropriate when overcoming some problem or obstacle has been identified as the main priority for a product or service: for example, giving a brand a new personality to keep up with changes in fashion (as when All-Bran was converted from a dull 'medicinal' brand into a 'healthy food'). It is 'indirect' because it is affecting not purchases directly so much as the mental climate within which purchasing choices are made.

Indirect 6. *Reinforce attitudes.* This is advertising to maintain the status quo: 'I always knew I was right to buy X'. Continuous advertising for package goods and much corporate advertising is like this. It confirms the *added values* which have been invested in the brand in the eyes of its buyers.

This direct-indirect scale is useful as a practical way of thinking about advertising objectives so as to prioritise them. It is not suggested that any advertisement only does one of these things; most advertisements work on several levels of directness. But the scale 'helps us to say what is the *main* role for advertising'.

The King Continuum contains clear echoes of James Webb Young, who worked at JWT for five decades and developed his ideas mostly as a copywriter in the twenties. He wrote, in *How to become an Advertising Man*[108] (which has been called one of the simplest and in some respects the best books ever written about advertising) that there were five ways in which advertising worked: by *familiarising*, by *reminding*, by *spreading news*, by *overcoming inertias*, and by *adding a value not in the product*. It is easy to see these five ideas surfacing at various points in King's direct-indirect scale: overcoming inertia at points 1 and 2, spreading news at point 3, reminding at point 4, adding values at points 5 and 6, familiarising throughout but especially at 4, 5 and 6.

A note about added values

It is customary to talk of these as something quite separate from the functional product, grafted on by the advertising in the process of turning a mere product into a brand. Persil is just any old soap powder until you *add* the values which make it Persil. 'A product is a physical thing, while a brand has no tangible, physical, or functional properties. Yet it is just as real as the product. Disembodied, abstract, ephemeral, it exists like a myth in the imagination of its consumer.' (Kim[65])

I am not sure that this rather disjunctive way of talking represents the real situation very satisfactorily: there is something spurious about the logic. It is difficult to think of a *purely* functional product. How would you define it? What aspects would you include as 'functional' and what exclude?

Suppose we have two soap powders which in blind tests seem to perform exactly the same. Imagine they were sold just as they stood, in meaningless uninformative packaging, the only difference being that they were identified as A and B. I suspect, indeed I would be willing to bet, that it would not be long before people started to invest A and B with characters. Perhaps retailers would start price-cutting A in response to a deal, so that A came to be seen as a cheaper buy. Perhaps B, for some people, would become the no-nonsense product that does the job, and they would get into the habit of using it and would start to feel it does the job particularly well. These are all values. Even to say a product is purely functional is to give it a value, of a sort: that is much what was done for Square Deal Surf. Own label products have value, because they are branded with the image of the retailer, which may be good or bad.

Rather than value being 'added' by advertising, it is more accurate to say that everything in a market has a value, which may be good or bad, given it by consumers, who will somehow organise the available options into preferential sets to suit themselves. It is consumers and their habit-forming tendencies who create branding; branding is inseparable from the ability to choose. What advertising does is to help *control* the acquisition of value, and give it a direction. If we did not advertise, our product would still acquire a 'branding', but it might not be one that we would like.

Bullmore[21] quotes James Webb Young[108] making a similar point, referring to the brand values as 'subjective': 'The truth ... is that – whether advertising exists or not – people add subjective values to alternative products themselves. They always have and they always will.' Young goes on: 'This use of advertising – to add a subjective value to the product – becomes increasingly important as the trends in our technology lead to competing products becoming more and more alike.'

Should we, perhaps, drop the 'added' from 'added values' and speak simply of brand values or 'brand equity', acknowledging that advertising is a major, but not the only, contributor to this?

High and low involvement: thinking and feeling

King's direct-indirect scale of responses is one useful framework for thinking about how we want people to react to our advertising. But no one, including I am sure JWT, would wish to argue that it is the only fruitful way. Human responses can be seen from all sorts of different angles, all of which are equally 'correct'. Probably every agency has its own favourite approach.

One worth mentioning, which has been well publicised, is the FCB Grid developed at the agency Foote, Cone & Belding (Berger[6], see also Vaughn[105,106]). This conceptualises the different psychological responses which the same people will use in different circumstances. It had been recognised for some time[64] that the logical and rational thought-processes described in hierarchy of effects models like DAGMAR or AIDA only applied to a limited set of purchase decisions; at other times, people respond to their senses, rely on intuition, or act by habit without giving thought to it at all. Before that, Krugman[72] had made the point that consumers are often not greatly 'involved' with the products they buy: they 'do not watch television or read magazines in order to make decisions about what brand of toothpaste or dog-food to buy next' (Joyce[63]).

These perceptions intensified as advertising people became more aware of psychological and neurological theory, including the distinction between left and right brain: the left being conscious, analytic and verbal, the right unconscious, intuitive and symbolic.

It is worth making the point here that a 'low-involvement' product, which people do not spend a long time thinking about, does not mean that the advertising has to be boring. Bullmore[21] says that the man who invented the term 'low interest product' performed one of the greatest disservices to the advertising business, because 'by inventing it, he provided the excuse for a lot of low interest advertising.' Any product is capable of being interesting at the time when someone needs it; if it seems dull, it is most likely because of the advertising. A genuinely dull product does not deserve to sell in the first place, and almost certainly won't.

The FCB Grid distinguishes four quadrants, according to whether the predominant responses are 'think' or 'feel', and whether the products are high or low involvement (Figure 4). Examples of each category are:

— *Think/high involvement*: choosing a camera, or a life insurance policy. Customers will seek information, compare features and prices, think about and take care over their choice. The mental sequence is Learn, then Feel, then Do, as with the hierarchy of effects approaches.

— *Think/low involvement*: not major purchases, therefore not requiring effort; but they do not give personal satisfaction; we are only interested if they work. It would be common to try a product on spec and see if it does the job required before we continue buying it. Examples might be household cleaners or petfoods. The sequence is Do-Learn-Feel.

— *Feel/high involvement*: an expensive perfume or fashion accessory; possibly cars or houses as well, although they require thought as well as emotional attraction, and straddle the think/feel line. The sequence is Feel-Learn-Do.

— *Feel/low involvement*: buying a Mars Bar or a pint of lager. The sequence is Do-Feel-Learn. Habits formed in response to social pressures will often come in here.

	THINK	FEEL
	Economic	Psychological
HIGH INVOLVEMENT	Learn-Feel-Do	Feel-Learn-Do
	Responsive	Social
LOW INVOLVEMENT	Do-Learn-Feel	Do-Feel-Learn

It is said that consumers' perceptions of what they are doing when they are buying different products fit onto this grid, often more to the right than had been thought, and that the patterns have been confirmed by research questions designed to elicit these perceptions and match across several countries. Again, the agency has found this grid helpful as a device for strategic thinking. It is easy to see that it is not opposed to the King Continuum, but could perfectly well be combined with it: one is about what we expect people to do, the other about whether we are appealing to thoughts or feelings. Some of King's categories, but not necessarily all, could be naturally distributed around this grid.

This grid is claimed to have been validated in the USA by constructing scales to measure the two axes of involvement and 'think-feel' and using them to rate some 250 product fields, some of which are shown below (Figure 5 from Joyce[63]).

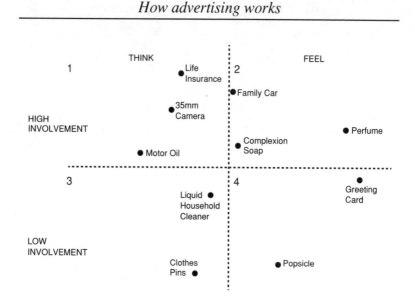

But again, its chief value is probably as a framework for concentrating thinking: what sort of product are we dealing with, and what sort of response should be looked for? Other grids of a similar type have been concocted for their own use by different advertising agencies.

How to be involved
What does 'involvement' mean?

Consideration of the FCB Grid introduces the notion of *emotional involvement*. Gordon Brown has argued convincingly in many papers, when talking of repeat purchase packaged products, that to ensure success an advertisement must *involve* prospects with the brand, and that many highly noticeable and attractive advertisements fail because, although they remain strongly in the memory, it is not in a way which links that memory clearly with the brand. In his most recent writing[20], he advances the view that this brand-linked involvement remains dormant until recalled into active memory by a relevant event, such as seeing the brand in the store when one is about to make a purchase. Long-term branding is thus a function of long-term *memory*, and the purpose of advertising for such brands is to keep this memory alive.

When using a term like 'involvement' one must beware, as always when discussing advertising, of seeming to imply too much. 'Emotional involvement' is not to be taken as meaning a high *intensity* of feeling. As Krugman[72] and many others since have pointed out, many purchases are low involvement. We are suggesting that advertising which is only fleetingly attended to may still 'involve'. As Krugman put it in a later article[70]: 'Quick and/or faint perceptions of advertising, even unremembered, do their job in most cases... (print) ads are meant to be looked at, to communicate as quick as a wink... the example of television is even more striking... commercials can get shorter and shorter and still do a job for the advertisers.'

Brown's thesis is that people are telling the truth when they claim in interviews that they are not influenced by advertising. When they see it on television, they are prone to be sceptical, and they are not in a decision-making mode. But when shopping, they may well be open to experimentation or 'trying something different for a change' and may then remember advertising; alternatively, advertising in some residual way may come into the mind in support of continuing a simplifying habit. In this way, repeated advertising, creatively renewed, is seen to have its main role in maintaining the buying habit; the view is consistent with all we know about stationary markets, including the fact that users have clearer and stronger images of brands (and brand values) than non-users do, and the fact that even new campaigns for well established successful brands frequently do *not* show up in short-term sales effects which are anything like great enough to justify the advertising expenditure.

Familiarising
How is the desired 'involvement' achieved? Brown[20] suggests

three mechanisms. One is 'immediate challenge', in which something new and interesting is suggested which catches the attention: difficult to achieve very often, but capable of having dramatic sales effects (as when Lucozade was re-presented as a drink for sportsmen). The second he calls 'interest-status': interest keeps an idea alive through a combination of curiosity and enjoyment of the familiar and loved (the continuing adventures of the PG chimps, or the Hofmeister bear, or the Oxo family); status ensures that a brand is safe, approved and fashionable, the one it is OK to use. The third mechanism is 'enhancement', in which, Brown suggests, advertising claims and images are 'converted, during experience of the product, into beliefs about the brand'. A vivid advertising memory may enhance perceptions that, for example, Gold Blend coffee has a 'quality' taste or a shampoo leaves the hair with 'natural body'. Enhancement happens, not when the advertising is seen, but when the brand is looked at or used.

These suggestions are not so much new ideas as helpful re-statements of old ones. James Webb Young[108] considered that one of the main purposes of advertising, indeed its fundamental role, was to make the brand 'familiar' or 'famous': the mechanisms above could be seen as ways of achieving 'fame'. The difficult thing to conceptualise is not how to make a brand familiar for the first time, but how to deal with it when it is *already* familiar – how to stop it becoming stale. We are back with the problem of the brand equity already achieved. Krugman[71], thinking about measuring responses to stimuli, suggested that 'familiar stimuli are not arousing simply because they have already been learned, that there is no further work to be done'; the work of the communication is done when the stimulus has lost excitement, when the response has returned to rest or 'some form of plateau.' Following this idea, one can think of the task for established advertising as repetition (to renew a faded memory) but in a way which *refreshes*, by presenting the familiar theme in newly interesting ways. Again one thinks of examples like the PG Tips chimpanzees, or the Oxo family.

Liking – in all its senses

Brown advances these ideas as hypotheses only and would not, I am sure, wish to suggest that they are necessarily comprehensive. But they make sense, in relation to the other things we know. One fact which seems to fit in well is the finding from the Advertising Research Foundation study, first reported in July 1990, that *whether a commercial is liked* appears to be the best predictor of sales (Biel[8]). Two previous studies by the WPP (previously the Ogilvy) Center for Research and Development, showed that liking appeared to be positively related to persuasion, as measured by a preference shift technique. The ARF study compared a range of copy testing methods by measuring against short term sales, using IRI split cable single source panels. To everyone's surprise, it was found that a simple liking scale proved to be a better predictor of sales than any other method, predicting winners 87% of the time. It seems from this that if people like an advertisement, they will become involved with it, very much the Brown hypothesis.

It is important not to misinterpret 'liking'. It does not necessarily mean *enjoyment*: it is not suggested that advertising must be entertaining. For some advertising subjects, AIDS or cancer research for example, 'entertainment' would be plainly inappropriate. It might have been more accurate, if less elegant, to have written at the end of the last paragraph: 'if people find an advertisement meaningful to them, they will become involved with it.'

One can 'like' something for all sorts of reasons: because it intrigues, because it satisfies curiosity, because it expresses feelings with which one identifies deeply, and so on, as well because it amuses. Biel, from a factor analysis of the detail from the second Ogilvy Center study, identified five 'factors' of likeability: ingenuity (amusing, clever, etc), 'meaningfulness' (worth remembering, true-to-life, convincing, etc.), warmth (gentle, sensitive, etc.), 'energy' (lively, fast-moving, appealing, etc), and 'rubs the wrong way' (a negative factor, consisting of 'seen a lot', worn-out, familiar, phony and irritating)[8].

Biel suggests a number of possible explanations of why 'liking' may be relevant to success: commercials that are liked are watched more; advertising is part of the brand's personality, so that if it is liked, it rubs off on the brand; good advertising 'entices the consumer into mental collaboration' (Bullmore[22]); enjoyable advertising evokes 'gratitude' on the part of the consumer, etc. Liking cannot, of course, be the only criterion: people can always find examples of advertising which is liked doing badly and advertising which is disliked being effective. As Brown would put it, whatever is liked in the advertising must enhance the brand, and not be irrelevant to it, if it is to do any good.

What is perhaps most surprising about this finding is the extent to which it appears to have surprised so many people. In the ARF Key Issues Workshop on the topic, September 1991[3], one academic paper (Thorson[104]) made a revealing comment that 'academic research on advertising was wedded to the idea that people's cognitive, rational beliefs about brands drove brand attitude and purchase. The idea that something so illogical as likeability was driving brand response was untenable.' This was why earlier academic evidence of the importance of likeability had to be replicated 'many times' over the past ten years to be taken seriously. In the same conference, Haley[42] made the point that almost none of the copy testing systems in vogue in the United States at the time of the study included measures of likeability, although 'to the credit of the copy research firms almost all are now doing some kind of research on likeability.' In Britain, the predictive importance of liking and emotive factors for assessing whether an advertisement was going to work as intended seems to have been accepted much earlier by advertising researchers, who have used them at least as diagnostic factors for many years.

We shall return to the subject of 'liking' in connection with copy-testing below. For the moment, the point to make is that it is clearly important and is complex: 'liking' may mean very different things and be expressed in many different ways.

Response functions: build up and wearout

This may be the right point for a small digression. It has long been customary to believe that, with repetition, advertising rapidly reaches a saturation point; that there are diminishing returns of 'effectiveness'. There are also arguments about whether advertising achieves its strongest effects immediately, and then begins to tail off, or whether, conversely, the first effects are slow and it builds up to a peak effectiveness before starting to diminish. These alternatives have been conceptualised as 'response functions' which can take one of two shapes: either a diminishing, concave curve, or an S-shaped curve which is convex to start with and then becomes concave.

These considerations are important, since when they are translated into computer models of media reach and frequency the assumptions made can have a large effect on spending. If three exposures or more, say, have little more effect than two, why pay for three, especially when media costs are rising all the time? But if at least two exposures are needed to reach peak effectiveness, we must ensure that many.

One of the main problems in discussing this area is the need to be extremely clear about the definition of the terms being used. By 'response' do you mean sales/probability of purchase, or some other measure? Are you talking about actual, proved exposures to advertisements, or 'opportunities to see' (which may merely mean that the advertisement was shown in a time slot when a set was recorded as switched on, and with luck the person in question was in the room at the time)? Another vital question is the time frame: are we interested in responses occurring within a day, a week, a month, or at the time of the next purchase (whenever that is), or what? All these could alter the values which we might feed into a computer model. And we have to remember that we are discussing something that occurs not in isolation but in a continuum. If response tails off after three or more exposures, we would not expect that effect to be permanent; if advertising is renewed later, after a lapse of time, would one not expect it to have a 'new' effect?

There seems to be very good evidence that saturation occurs. Simon and Arndt[98], after a wide ranging review of available evidence, concluded that virtually all the studies showed that there were diminishing returns of sales to advertising, whether one looked at it in unit or dollar terms, but that there was no evidence of an S-shaped curve. Krugman explained it in psychological terms, based on laboratory experiment using eye-movement measures: two or three exposures were the optimum level for receipt of a message because:

— the *first* exposure has to be taken in; the reaction is 'What is it?', and there has to be just enough response to decide whether to pay attention or to block out the message;

— the *second* exposure is recognised with the reaction 'What of it?'; more detail may be taken in at this stage with the feeling 'Is this relevant to me?';

— the *third* exposure reminds, the task of noting and taking in the message having been done; but it is also the beginning of disengagement, or withdrawal of attention from a completed task;

— subsequent exposures can do no more than call back to mind in the same way as the third exposure; they cannot *add* anything;

— but if more exposures are seen after a lapse of time, they may be seen freshly *as if they were the second*; the recipient forgets the evaluation he made before and is therefore led to *remake* it.

Thus, Krugman's account implies that satiation occurs after two or three exposures in a short space of time, but also the possibility of later renewal[73]. Other well known experiments pointed in the same direction[38, 39, 109].

This passage from Krugman introduces the notion of wearout, or saturation, as a psychological, not just a behavioural matter. It is not simply that, whether one sees an advertisement once or ten times, one can only buy the brand so much; we are now considering how long it takes to strike home to us (wearin), and how soon we become bored with it because it is familiar. This suggests in turn that the real response function (as opposed to the artefact constructed for media scheduling purposes) has much capacity to vary according to the copy, the subject, the target audience, etc. Haley[42] suggests that likeability is a predictor of wearout: 'the seeds of wearout are embedded in the copy, and ... likeability measures can do a far better job of identifying wearout potential than can persuasion and recall scores – especially in one and two exposure testing.'

The place of copy testing
Prediction or diagnosis?
King's direct-indirect response scale and the FCB Grid, and other similar systems, are practical devices for helping one to think in a coherent manner about what one should be trying to do in a particular advertising campaign, the nature of the response to be sought. They are guidelines based on experience, and the evidence for them remains firmly anecdotal. But they are in no sense a 'how to do it' blueprint for writing the copy

that will achieve the involvement with the brand, or whatever else is desired. Each advertisement must still be a unique creative achievement.

Advertisers need to be able to assess whether their advertisement is likely to achieve the desired result, preferably before they have spent too much money producing it. Copy testing (or advertisement pre-testing) has therefore been part of the scene for many years. As everyone knows, it has been, and remains, highly controversial. All methods of pre-testing advertising, however carefully designed, are in some sense artificial: the advertising is not seen or heard as it would be in real life, and the responses sought, through questionnaires or discussions, are induced by an interviewer, not occurring naturally. It is therefore not clear and obvious how to interpret them. In the absence of general, objective agreement, several different approaches and measurement systems have grown up and have established their validity largely by compiling 'norms', ie sets of cases showing the average and range of scores expected for each measure, against which new examples can be compared. Clients have adopted the system they feel comfortable with. Validation in terms of the end product, sales, has been generally unavailable, until the arrival of single-source data made possible the ARF's Copy Research Validity Project (CRVP), to which a brief reference has already been made.

Underlying the disagreements about which method to use is the tension between the different objectives of the advertiser and the agency: the advertiser wanting reassurance that his spending will be productive, the agency shrinking from having its creative scope put at the mercy of a limited and insensitive measurement and, at worst, its best ideas killed off. Agencies often argue that there can be no standard 'template' for advertising, and that the real value of pre-testing research is to help in the development of the advertisement, which is usually best done by qualitative methods under the agency's control.

It seems to me that the basic and really interesting divergence in attitudes to copy testing is not whether it should be quantitative or qualitative, or whether recall, persuasion or something else is more important, or even the tension between advertiser and agency, although it relates to all of these. The important distinction is between those who see the purpose of testing as *predicting sales effectiveness* (ie, are only concerned about the end result, not about how to get there), and those who see it as *diagnostic* (ie, something to help one produce better advertising). Many, of course, would claim to have both objectives; the distinction is between two intellectual positions, not necessarily between groups of people.

The difference reminds one of that noted earlier between the two theories of the 'passive' and 'active' consumer. Predictive methods which rely on pre-post exposure shifts to a normative level, in recall ('clutter awareness') or persuasion (in terms of some measure of expressed preference) are closely allied to 'passive' causal models and to the idea of a hierarchy of effects: there is the same sort of chain between the advertisement being noticed, the object being understood and desired, and purchases to follow; and there is the same implication that the receivers will respond in a uniform way. A diagnostic approach, on the other hand, is intensely concerned about the different ways people respond, and why they think and feel as they do. And, just as the emphasis has swung over the years from the 'passive' to the 'active' consumer, so diagnostic considerations have become more important in copy testing. The ARF Workshop in 1991[3], which discussed industry reactions to the Copy Research Validity Project (CRVP), provided plentiful evidence of this, including comments in papers given by representatives of leading copy-testing systems based on awareness and persuasion shifts (eg Peter Klein of McCollum Spielman[68] entitled his paper: 'Evaluative v. diagnostic: do you have to make a choice?'). Another paper (Spaeth and Feldman[100]) underlined the shift of emphasis: 'Traditionally, advertising researchers have looked at evaluative and diagnostic testing techniques as separate and distinct. Diagnostic techniques weren't believed to be useful for evaluation and evaluative techniques often weren't terribly insightful, diagnostically. This may have been the accepted tradition in our industry, but it doesn't make much sense at all.'

The ARF Copy Research Validity Project

The ARF CRVP broke new ground by being able to compare copy testing methods against actual sales results, thanks to single-source data from IRI. Even though the sample of commercials was small, the results were striking. Five pairs of commercials for the same FMCG brand were chosen; in each pair, one commercial had performed notably better than the other, in sales terms, in an IRI split cable test. Each pair was run through the six main copy testing methods. The results showed that measures of 'likeability' distinguished best between the more and less successful commercial in each pair, but that 'persuasion' and 'recall' also worked well; indeed, there is a large degree of correlation between the various measures (but beware here especially the 'research naming fallacy' we warned against on p. 13). They also showed that it appears to make no difference whether test respondents see the commercials off-air (in a laboratory) or on-air, in single or multiple exposures, or are interviewed only after exposure as opposed to pre-post, thus apparently disposing of a number of traditional worries relating to copy testing's supposed 'artificiality'. To judge from the commentary at the ARF Workshop, no-one thinks that these results have set a simple copy testing standard. What they have done is to raise productive questions about, for example, what can be meant by 'likeability', recognisably a complex of attitudes and feelings, and what the relationship is between 'likeability' and persuasion, etc.

The limits of prediction

The CRVP appears to have shown that copy testing methods work, but in what sense exactly? Does it mean that we can safely use copy testing to predict sales results? From IRI's 'How Advertising Works' report, it would appear not. This report concluded that 'the relationship between standard recall and persuasion scores and the sales impact for established brands is tenuous, at best.' (Lubetkin[80])

This paradox is easily reconcilable. The CRVP worked back to front: it took pairs of commercials which had already achieved large sales differences, and found that the copy test results correlated with these. Clearly, no other factors beyond control had intervened in the form of competitor activity, distribution problems, bad media buying etc. It is possible that a good copy test result is a necessary condition for eventual success, although this still needs proving – perhaps it is safer to call it a reassuring condition – but it is certainly not sufficient.

It is important to be clear about the limits of what we can achieve when we pre-test an advertisement before letting it loose on the market. I remember the gentleman who said at an *Admap* conference on pre-testing that the reason the audience were all there was 'the failure of all pre-testing methods to predict sales'[81]. But, even with split cable single-source panel tests, where the advertising is exposed in a more controlled manner than normal, predicting sales is an unreasonable expectation; too many other things can happen.

What pre-testing *can* do, with varying success, is to give us a basis for making a better judgement of whether the advertisement is *likely* to perform as intended, if all the other things which we cannot control go well. This is a perfectly valid mental activity, which we engage in when we buy most products which cost real money: we cannot predict that our new car will not break down, or that the house we are buying will not suffer from subsidence or planning blight, but we can do a great deal to reassure ourselves that it is *unlikely*, other things being equal.

We would rightly call this activity 'diagnostic', and, from this angle, the distinction drawn earlier between diagnostic and predictive attitudes is a false one: to diagnose *is* to predict; one cannot do one without the other. The lesson from projects like the CRVP is that we have to abandon thinking of advertising as a 'black box' in whose workings we have no interest so long as they produce a result. Understanding the workings is a prerequisite for looking forward to a result. It should not need saying in this context that this process of diagnosis is not only, or even necessarily, qualitative, but also has an important place for statistical statements about the ways *populations* or target groups respond.

How to improve diagnosis

This shift towards interest in diagnosis is showing up the place where there is still a serious gap in our ability to understand advertising. This is that we do not analyse the *structure* of the advertisement on any theoretical basis to look for inherent strengths and weaknesses. We lack the framework for doing so. Because of this, it is difficult, although we constantly try to do it, to take an advertisement apart in detail and say: 'because of these features here, we can anticipate that the likely response of Y target group will be X', or 'that way of putting it will mean that the message we want people to get will be obscured, but if we turned it around this way, the obstacle should disappear.' Diagnosis of this kind *involves* prediction, and would naturally carry with it the whole hierarchy of evaluative research from qualitative experimenting to pre-testing to eventual market-place tests. The trouble is that, because we have no theory to help us, we tend to interpret the content of advertisements in an anecdotal way, or in terms of our own instinctive emotional responses. This is by no means necessarily wrong, but it leaves too great an uncertainty: it is at the bottom of why ads which are enjoyed by other advertising men and win awards some-times prove disappointing in the marketplace, and why at worst we have often been able to predict potential success only by reference to 'norms' obtained for other brands, perhaps in quite different product fields. We have moved some way from relying on scores without knowing the reason for them, but not yet far enough.

Before I am lynched by a close formation of creatives, let me make one thing clear at this point. There is absolutely nothing in what is being discussed here which would inhibit creative freedom. On the contrary, it would be enhanced enor-mously. At present, copywriters have to rely on their own commonsense understanding of humanity, which for all of us is imperfect, and on practitioners' words of wisdom aided by thinking frameworks like those discussed earlier. With a better theoretical understanding they would be working with a new, sharpened set of tools compared to the blunt old ones they use now. Being able to question their own work more easily against this knowledge, they could be more, not less, confident in experimenting.

This absence of an academic basis for analysing the content of advertisements is a remaining black hole, and probably the next one to be tackled by the industry: it is where we ought to expect progress over the next few years. This is certainly the direction in which some papers at the ARF Workshop on copy research were looking. For instance, an academic paper by Kover[69] spoke of observations he had made into the complexity of how viewers respond to television messages, challenging Krugman's designation of it as a 'low involvement' medium; he was looking not only at how people learn or are affected, but how they *resist* those changes, often very strongly; how, when their attention is engaged, their involvement is high. Another significant comment came from an advertiser (Richard Nelson of Campbell Soup Company[86]). His concern was what to do about the advertisement which fails to perform well in a test. This puts the company in a dilemma: they do not want to waste money by putting a failing ad on air; equally, shifting the money to promotions is a counsel of despair; but usually there is no alternative creative treatment available, and no funds or time available to make one. Nelson goes on to raise the question: how can we fix the execution we have? 'Several services provide an opinion on whether or not an execution contains certain elements known to be related to effective communication and good persuasion. My question is, how far do these insights go in helping you fix the execution?' And later: 'Let's return to the dilemma of what should be done when the spot doesn't test well. The answer is still to fix it. But how? Few of the presentations I've been to or reports that I've read have offered specific creative direction. Why? Are we lacking the analytic expertise …?' Later still in Nelson's paper is the following telling quotation, which shows this advertiser's awareness of precisely where the black hole is:

'Let me sum up how I feel we are doing on developing superior advertising. When it comes to telling marketing what happened on a particular execution, I feel we're doing a good job. And, as I said earlier, my issue is not validity. I feel more emphasis needs to be placed on how we can make executions more productive, and that virtually no one is successfully doing this today. Then, getting the client to buy into what's wrong and how it can be addressed is something virtually no one is doing. *To do that you need to do solid analysis and put it into a persuasive presentation. It's also, I feel, an opportunity for a whole new industry.*' ([86] - my italics)

A place for communication theory?

One obvious way of developing the missing theory of advertising responses is through *communication theory*. It seems strange that there has been so little academic attempt to apply communication theory to advertising, with rare exceptions such as Krugman's proposals for the laboratory study of communication response[70]. Communication theory has links with, and would suck in, a range of disciplines to do with how the mind and body work: anthropology, neurology, psychology, cybernetics, linguistics, to name but a few. There is substantial knowledge already available to be drawn on.

For example, quite a lot is known now about how the human brain processes information, about the way that a message can be distorted in the process of reception so that what is eventually received is different from what was transmitted, etc. We are beginning to learn about *the basic patterns of thinking and feeling*, which are limited in number, and about how people switch between them; how these patterns are grounded in our neurological make-up and operate both in the right-brain (intuitive, overview) mode and in the left-brain (analytic, attention-to-detail) mode. There is also evidence beginning to appear that people differ in their thinking habits, and that these relate to the choices they make. The next stage of progress might well be to develop procedures for analysing advertisements in detail to see how effectively, or not, they *use the capacity of the brain to absorb and respond to communications of different kinds*. As Krugman put it: 'structure in the stimulus elicits structure in the response.'[70]. In this way, one might have solid grounds for telling in advance how likely a particular communication is to 'involve' people (even down to a line of copy or a frame), because we would know more about the mechanisms of 'involvement', what opens the communication channels and what, conversely, sets up blockages. We could, if we obtained such knowledge, see more easily whether the component parts of an advertisement (or a campaign in different media) were complementing each other so as to multiply the total effect, or were negating each other and spoiling the effect.

This is one approach, and no doubt there will be others. The strength of advertising is that its development has been driven by its practitioners over the years. I am suggesting now that this strength has become a point of weakness, and there is need for a new academic input into the subject. It will not replace creativity, judgement or the need for evaluative research, but it will make these activities (if we achieve it) much more productive than they are now. At this stage in the evolution of advertising, we should be able to say with much greater confidence *why* advertisements succeed or fail, as well as *that* they do.

Summary: what kinds of response are possible?

1. Advertising is enormously varied. Every new advertisement is a unique creative activity. Yet several successful practitioners have developed *ways of thinking, or 'rules of thumb'*, which have worked for them and which they pass on in books. Two examples are given for illustration: the J. Walter Thompson scale of desired response (from direct action to reinforcing attitudes), which helps to decide what the primary role of the advertising is going to be, and the Foote, Cone and Belding Grid, a matrix which relates the two dimensions of high- or low-involvement (for the purchase decision), and rational/emotional, or 'thinking' versus 'feeling' (for the response expected).

2. The hypothesis is discussed that advertising, at least for low-involvement, repeat-purchase products, may work by involving people with the brand, and that this *'involvement' becomes lodged in the long-term memory*, so that it comes to mind, or the effect is somehow felt, when that memory is triggered (eg, when actually shopping). People tell the truth when they say that they are not affected by advertising,

thinking of when they are watching it. This seems consistent with the old idea (from James Webb Young[108]) that the fundamental task for advertising is to make a brand *familiar*, and with the importance of *liking/interest/meaningfulness* for an advertisement's success.

3. There seems to be good evidence that advertising responses *build up and become saturated* (the 'concave response function'). But one has to be careful to define one's terms. Saturation can be seen as a fall-off in purchase probability after having opportunities to see a number of advertisements, if one is looking at single-source panel data, or it may be viewed in psychological terms, eg, Krugman's theory about the number of times one has to see an advertisement to fully grasp the message[73]. The timing also matters: after how long a gap does the familiar message seem fresh once more?

4. The ARF's Copy Research Validity Project appears to have shown that *copy testing methods are capable of discriminating* between commercials which are more or less successful in producing sales, and that measures of 'liking' (defined in the widest sense – not just enjoyment, but interest and relevance too) are at least as important as more traditional 'persuasion' and 'recall' measures. Copy testing cannot predict that sales success will happen, because there are too many uncontrolled influences besides the copy, but they have a more realistic and equally important function of *providing reassurance that the advertisement is likely to do the job required of it*, and will not be a waste of money. For this purpose, 'diagnosis', or understanding *why* the advertisement is likely to work well or badly, is at least as important as forecasting a result.

5. There has been a shift of emphasis over the years away from

'prediction' and towards 'diagnosis' as the perceived aim of copy testing; this has parallelled the swing away from the 'passive consumer', to whom advertising does things, to the 'active consumer', who uses advertising and discards the clutter. But we are not yet, as a whole, very good at diagnosis; we rely heavily on common-sense judgement, anecdote and normative comparisons. It is suggested that this is because we lack a theoretical basis against which to analyse the content of advertisements and interpret test findings. There are a number of academic disciplines, such as communication theory, which could usefully be applied to this problem, but with rare exceptions it has not been seriously attempted. The commercial justification for such an effort would be that it would give us greater confidence, not only in spotting what may be wrong with an advertisement, but knowing how to put it right.

7 The rules of the game

We started this review with the call, made by W. Henderson Pringle in 1932, for 'the acquisition of scientific knowledge over a wide field' in order to improve the practice of advertising.

It is clear that there is not, and almost certainly never will be, *a science* of advertising, in this hopeful sense. Advertising is not homogeneous enough to make that possible; and it is even more diverse now than it was in those days, as Winston Fletcher has pointed out[37]. What we appear to have is a very large collection of insights and accumulated skills; successful practitioners finding out what works for them and passing it on to others, sometimes through 'how to do it' books; a constantly developing influence from the social and cultural fashions of the time; and new technology, which enables advertisers to do ever more amazing (or, if you prefer, outrageous) things.

Nevertheless, things called 'advertising' must be expected to share some distinguishing features, which can provide a framework for thinking about it. If we can understand these features, it ought to be clear where the strengths and weaknesses of advertising are, where we are safest in relying on it and where we come up against its limitations.

We have been looking at a number of features of this kind. Briefly, we can list them as follows.

1. Advertising cannot expand markets indefinitely, or create new markets unless there is a latent unsatisfied demand. Although it may suggest ideas, it cannot compel people to act against their will.

2. Within a market, advertising is a powerful force in establishing and sustaining market share. It does this primarily by investing a brand with its own 'brand equity'. This 'equity' is maintained by a combination of continued

advertising and other franchise-building activities, and actual brand experience.

3. Advertising enables some brands to attain leading positions which are very hard to assail, and which can command premium prices; but it also fuels competition, and in so doing helps to stabilise markets and keep prices down.

4. As markets reach their natural equilibrium, as happens increasingly in developed economies when the capacity to use the product becomes saturated, the role of advertising in holding the dynamic balance between the competitors becomes more important.

5. Good advertising elicits an immediate response, but at the same time builds for the future: it is a continuing investment in the brand. In this it is distinct from many promotions, which do nothing to build brand franchise, and which sacrifice revenue for a temporary gain.

6. Plenty of evidence has now been seen that advertising can increase effective sales, including in the longer term, and that it can improve profits. 'Effective sales' should be (but too often is not) taken to mean not simply volume increase, but a price-volume combination which yields a satisfactory profit.

7. However, such sales effects of advertising are more easily seen when brands are new or markets are growing. In stable, competitive markets which have reached equilibrium, there is often no scope to expect sales increases, unless they are achieved at the expense of competitors' weakness. When a market is full of strong competitors in a dynamic balance, a failure to 'see' sales increases in the aggregate cannot be

taken as proof that the advertising is ineffective. To drop advertising in such cases may well result in 'death of the brand'.

8. The problem of distinguishing between advertising which is working effectively in such established, balanced markets and advertising which is ineffective is the major challenge confronting advertising effectiveness research. It applies not only to sales but to other measures of response, such as brand images, brand awareness and advertising awareness.

9. This problem cannot be solved by looking for aggregate measures of change, because these, by definition, will tend to be hard to find. It requires more detailed analysis, which focusses on observing change within individuals: behaviourally through single-source data analysed within person over time, attitudinally through better diagnosis of the mental and emotional responses to the advertisement.

10. Whether we prefer to see people as 'passive' or 'active' recipients of advertising, they will only respond to what is relevant to them at the time. For most people, most of the time, that condition will not apply, and the increasing variety of advertising opportunities is making this situation worse. This puts a premium on targeting, not only of people, but of occasions and moods; not only in how to reach them, but in how to speak to them.

11. There is reason to think that successful advertising involves people with the brand in some way, perhaps implanting a memory which is activated only when the time is relevant. 'Liking', in its widest sense (ie not just enjoyment, but interest or relevance) has been shown to be an important factor. But the ability to diagnose just what it is that makes

a particular execution able to attract a desired response has not yet been developed into a very fine art.

12. The place for copy testing is not to predict sales success directly, but to forecast the capability of the advertisement to attract the desired response assuming that all other influences are equal. This is increasingly seen as a matter of good diagnosis. But, here again, there are few guides to judgement beyond anecdote and reliance on normative data, not necessarily from relevant measures.

If these common features of advertising are agreed, there are certain implications; we may perhaps get some old preoccupations out of the way, and set an agenda for the future.

1. We surely do not have to go on demonstrating that 'advertising', in general terms, can work to influence sales and market share. There is plenty of published evidence from a wide range of examples.

2. Marketers are not, of course, interested in generalities but in their own particular case: is their advertising investment justified? The task here is to clarify what will demonstrate success in different cases. It is no good looking for sales increases in conditions where it is unreasonable to expect to find them. One needs to develop measures which are relevant, eg, through better use of single-source data.

3. Marketers should be urged to stop setting their goals in terms of volume increase or market share, without reference to the long-term health of brands or the cost of the sales gained in lost revenue. As Jones has demonstrated[60], it is possible to calculate advertising and price elasticities and thus work out the effect on profits of assumed effects on

sales from price-cutting as opposed to franchise-building activities.

4. There is a need to develop more *detailed* analyses, of behaviour and of attitudinal responses, to understand under what conditions advertising becomes *most* effective. This covers issues like timing and frequency, *competitive* weight, how advertising interacts with other franchise-building activities such as consumer promotions, how advertising in different media interact with each other, etc. It also, of course, involves understanding what constitutes one's own, and competitors', 'brand equity' or 'added value'.

5. There is a need to develop a better framework of knowledge for *diagnosis* of how a particular advertisement is likely to work and interpretation of copy tests. We have suggested that this is now an area ripe for the serious application of academic disciplines such as communication theory.

6. If the first conclusion above is accepted, that advertising does not force people to do what they don't want to do, we ought to be able to dispose of the political dilemma raised in the introduction. Advertising works strongly in its proper area, of enabling brand choices to be made; for changing overall habits, whether they are commercial or social, it can go no faster than peoples' willingness to change. It can help to persuade (as shown, for example, by the AAAA's 'Partnership for a Drug-Free America' campaign[90]), but only when it interacts with social movements in the same direction: there is likely in such cases to be a hard core who resist change and easily shut out the advertising.

    In such circumstances, the weak logic of, for example, governments who seek to curtail an activity which is thought to be undesirable, such as smoking tobacco, by banning advertising but leaving the activity itself untouched, is revealed clearly. A demand for a legally available product (even an illegal one if the demand is strong enough) will be satisfied somehow. How can it make sense to pick on advertising but leave the production and distribution of the product itself untouched? Unfortunately, advertising is an easy target for those whose main objective is to satisfy political pressure. It would be both fairer and more effective to *use* advertising to put across the counter view, so that the anti-social activity, whatever it is, will come to be seen as unfashionable or socially unacceptable.

7. Finally, advertising can be seen, shorn of misconceptions, for what it is: neither a wimp nor an ogre, but a generator of real value if used in the right way. For all the difficulty of targeting those who will attend to it, advertising still remains, as Winston Fletcher has put it[37]: 'an exceedingly economical form of mass communication... infinitely less expensive than most of its competitors... easily the most cost-effective means of reaching millions and millions of unknown people, some of whom are, or may become, customers.'

Bibliography

NB: Place of publication is London, unless otherwise stated.

1.   Abraham, M.M. & Lodish, L.M., 'Fact-based Strategies for Managing Advertising and Promotion Dollars: Lessons from Single-Source Data', Working Paper No.89-035, Pennsylvania, Wharton School, University of Pennsylvania, 1989.

2.   Abraham, M.M. & Lodish, L.M., 'Getting the Most Out of Advertising and Promotion', *Harvard Business Review*, v.68(3), May-June 1990, pp.50-60.

3.   Advertising Research Foundation, 'Copy Research: the New Evidence', Proceedings of the 8th Annual ARF Copy Research Workshop, New York: Advertising Research Foundation, September 1991.

4.   Baker, C., 'The Evaluation of Advertising Effects: Philosophy, Planning and Practice', *Admap*, v.20(4), No.227, April 1984, pp.192-199.

5.   Benham, L. 'The Effect of Advertising on the Price of Eyeglasses', *Journal of Law and Economics*, v.15(2), October 1972, pp.337-352.

6.   Berger, D., 'Theory into Practice: the FCB Grid', *European Research*, v.14(1), 1986, pp.35-46 (see also: Vaughn, D. refs. 105 & 106 for another account of the FCB planning model).

7.   Biel, A.L., 'Coping with Recession: Why budget-cutting may not be the answer', Keynote address to the3rd Advertising Research Foundation Advertising and Promotion Workshop, February 1991. In *It Works! How Investment Spending in Advertising Pays Off*, Ryan, B., New York, American

Association of Advertising Agencies, 1991.

8.   Biel, A.L., 'Love the Ad. Buy the Product? Why Liking the Advertising and Preferring the Brand Aren't Such Strange Bedfellows After All', *Admap*, v.26(9), No.299, September 1990, pp.21-25.

9.   Biel, A.L., 'Strong Brand, High Spend: Tracking Relationships Between the Marketing Mix and Brand Values', *Admap*, v.26(11), No.301, November 1990, pp.35-40. (see also: Ogilvy Centre for Research and Development, ref. 88)

10.   Biel, A.L., 'The Cost of Cutbacks', *Admap*, v.26(5), No.307, May 1991, pp.28-31.

11.   Bloom., D., 'Consumer Behaviour and the Timing of Advertising Effects', *Admap*, v.12(9), September 1976, pp.430-438.

12.   Bloom, D., 'Do We Need to Worry about Long-term Effects?', *Admap*, v.25(9), No.289, October 1989, pp.49-52.

13.   Borden, N.H., *The Economic Effects of Advertising*, Chicago, Richard D. Irwin, 1942.

14.   Broadbent, S., 'Modelling with Adstock', *Journal of the Market Research Society*, v.26(4), October 1984, pp.295-312.

15.   Broadbent, S., 'Using Data Better: a New Approach to Sales Analyses', *Admap*, v.27(1), No.314, January 1992, pp.48-54.

16.   Broadbent, S., 'Modelling Beyond the Blip', *Journal of the Market Research Society*, v.32(1), January 1990, pp.61-102.

17.   Broadbent, S., 'Price and Advertising: Volume and Profit', *Admap*, v.16(11), November 1980, p.536.

18. Broadbent, S., *The Advertising Budget. The Advertiser's Guide to Budget Determination,* Institute of Practitioners in Advertising/NTC Publications Ltd, 1989.

19. Broadbent, S., 'Two OTS in a Purchase Interval: Some Questions', *Admap,* v.22(11), No.257, November 1986, pp.12-16.

20. Brown, G., *How Advertising Affects the Sales of Packaged Goods Brands: a Working Hypothesis for the 1990s,* Warwick, Millward Brown International plc, 1991.

21. Bullmore, J., *Behind the Scenes in Advertising,* NTC Publications Ltd, Henley-on-Thames, 1991.

22. Bullmore, J., 'Getting Explicit About the Implicit', *Admap,* v.21(10), No.245, October 1985, pp.478-479.

23. Colley, R., *Defining Advertising Goals for Measured Advertising Results,* New York, Association of National Advertisers, 1961.

24. Cooper, C., Cook, L. & Jones, N., 'How the Chimps Have Kept PG Tips Brand LeaderThrough 35 Years of Intense Competition', In *Advertising Works 6. Papers from the IPA Advertising Effectiveness Awards, 1990,* (Ed) Feldwick, P. pp.3-25, NTC Publications Ltd, Henley-on-Thames, 1991.

25. Corlett, T., 'Anyone for Econometrics?', *Admap,* v.14(8), August 1978, pp.376-383.

26. Corlett, T., 'How We Should Measure the Longer-term Effects of Advertising on Purchasing', *Admap,* v.12(9), September 1976, pp.422-433.

27. Corlett, T., 'Modelling the Sales Effects of Advertising: Today's Questions', *Admap,* v.21(10), No.245, October 1985, pp.486-500.

28.   Dept. of National Health and Welfare, Health Protection Branch, Tobacco Products Unit, Rebuttal to a Brief Submitted to the Minister by the Institute of Canadian Advertising, Issued on May 25th, 1987, Ottawa, Dept. of National Health and Welfare, 1987.

29.   Ehrenberg, A.S.C., 'New Brands and the Existing Market', *Journal of the Market Research Society*, v.33(4), October 1991, pp.285-299.

30.   Ehrenberg, A.S.C., *Repeat-buying: Facts, Theory and Applications*, 2nd ed., New York, Oxford University Press, London: Charles Griffin, 1988.

31.   Ekelund, R.B. Jr. & Saurman, D.S., *Advertising and the Market Process: a Modern Economic View*, San Francisco, Pacific Research Institute for Public Policy, 1988.

32.   Elliott, J., 'How Advertising Frequency Affects Advertising Effectiveness: Indications of Change', *Admap*, v.21(10), No.245, October 1985, pp.512-515.

33.   Elliott, J., 'Kellogg's Rice Krispies: the Effect of a New Creative Execution', In *Advertising Works. Papers from the Advertising Effectiveness Awards, 1980*, (Ed) Broadbent, S., pp78-88, (especially chart on p84), Holt, Rinehart & Winston, 1981.

34.   Federal Trade Commission, Bureau of Consumer Protection, Eyeglasses II. Report of the Staff to the FTC and Recommendation on Proposed Trade Regulation Rule 16 CFR, Part 456, October 1986, pp.159-160. In *Ophthalmic Practice Rules*, US, FTC, 1986.

35.   Feldwick, P., 'Introduction', In *Advertising Works 6. Papers from the IPA Advertising Effectiveness Awards, 1990*, (Ed) Feldwick, P. pp.vii-xviii, NTC Publications Ltd, Henley-on-Thames, 1991.

36.   Feldwick, P., 'The Use (and Abuse) of Market Research in the Evaluation of Advertising Effect', Paper given at the 32nd MRS Conference, pp.276-286, Market Research Society, 1989.

37.   Fletcher, W., *A Glittering Haze: Strategic Advertising in the 1990s,* NTC Publications Ltd, Henley-on-Thames, 1992.

38.   Grass, R.C., 'Satiation Effects of Advertising', 14th Annual Conference, New York, Advertising Research Foundation, 1968.

39.   Grass, R.C. & Wallace, W.H., 'Satiation Effects of TV Commercials', *Journal of Advertising Research*, v.9(3), September 1969, pp.3-8.

40.   Greyser, S.A., California Avocado Advisory Board, In *Cases in Advertising and Communications Management*, 2nd ed., pp.23-61, Englewood Cliffs, New Jersey, Prentice-Hall, 1981. (Jones says that all the data he quotes comes from this source.)

41.   Gullen, P., 'Planning Media to Create Sales', *Admap*, v.21(10), No.245, October 1985, pp.505-511.

42.   Haley, R.J., 'Likeability: One Man's Opinion', Paper given at the 8th Annual ARF Copy Research Workshop - Copy Research: the New Evidence, New York, Advertising Research Foundation, September 1991.

43.   Hall, M. & Maclay, D., 'Science and Art: How Does Research Practice Match Advertising Theory?', Paper given at Market Research Society Conference, 1991.

44. Haselhurst, L., 'How Pedigree Petfoods Evaluate Their Advertising Spend', *Admap*, v.24(6), No.275, June 1988, pp.29-31.

45. Hedges, A., *Testing to Destruction*, Institute of Practitioners in Advertising, 1974.

46. Henry, H., 'Does Advertising Affect Total Market Size?', *Admap*, v.20(11), No.234, November 1984, pp.524-532.

47. Hopkins, C., *Scientific Advertising*, MacGibbon & Kee, 1968 (original text copyrighted in 1923).

48. Information Resources Inc., Brochure describing IRI BehaviorScan. Chicago, Illinois: I.R.I., autumn 1991.

49. Information Resources Inc., 'How Advertising Works: Management Summary', Chicago, Illinois, I.R.I., November 1991. (NB. The full report of this study is only available to its sponsors.)

50. *Advertising Works. Papers from the IPA Advertising Effectiveness Awards 1980*, (Ed) Broadbent, S., Holt, Rinehart & Winston, 1981.

51. *Advertising Works 2. Papers from the IPA Advertising Effectiveness Awards 1982*, (Ed) Broadbent, S., Holt, Rinehart & Winston, 1983.

52. *Advertising Works 3. Papers from the IPA Advertising Effectiveness Awards 1984*, (Ed) Channon, C., Holt, Rinehart & Winston, 1985.

53. *Advertising Works 4. Papers from the IPA Advertising Effectiveness Awards 1986*, (Ed) Channon, C., Cassell, 1987.

54. *Advertising Works 5. Papers from the IPA Advertising Effectiveness Awards 1988*, (Ed) Feldwick, P., Cassell, 1990.

55. *Advertising Works 6. Papers from the IPA Advertising Effectiveness Awards 1990,* (Ed) Feldwick, P., NTC Publications Ltd, Henley-on-Thames, 1991.

56. Jenkins, E. & Timms, C., 'The Andrex Story – a Soft, Strong and Very Long-term Success', In *Advertising Works 4. Papers from the IPA Advertising Effectiveness Awards, 1986,* (Ed) Channon, C., pp.179-190, Cassell, 1987.

57. Jones, J.P., 'Advertising and the Economic System', Appendix A in *How Much is Enough? Getting the Most from Your Advertising Dollar,* New York, Lexington Books/Macmillan. To be published June 1992.

58. Jones, J.P., *Does It Pay to Advertise? Cases Illustrating Successful Brand Advertising,* Indianapolis, Lexington Books, 1989.

59. Jones, J.P., 'Advertising: Strong or Weak Force? Two Views an Ocean Apart', *International Journal of Advertising,* v.9(3), 1990, pp.233-246. (NB. Another version of the same paper is published under the title: 'Over-promise and Under-delivery', *Marketing & Research Today,* v.19(4), November 1991, pp.195-203.)

60. Jones, J.P., 'The Double Jeopardy of Sales Promotions', *Harvard Business Review,* v.68(5), September-October 1990, pp.145-152.

61. Jones, J.P., *What's in a Name? Advertising and the Concept of Brands,* Indianapolis, Lexington Books, 1986.

62. Joyce, T., 'Adding Print Exposures to Single Source Data Bases', Paper given at the ARF Seminar – Breakthrough Marketplace Advertising Research for Bottom Line Results, New York, Advertising Research Foundation, November 1991.

63. Joyce, T., 'Models of the Advertising Process', In *How Advertising Works and How Promotions Work*, pp.267-281, ESOMAR Seminar in Amsterdam, 22-24 April 1991, Amsterdam, ESOMAR, 1991.

64. Joyce, T., 'What Do We Know About How Advertising Works?' In *Market Researchers Look at Advertising. A Collection of ESOMAR Papers 1949-1979,* (Ed) Broadbent, S. pp.27-38, Sigmatext, 1980. (NB. Originally published by J. Walter Thompson, 1967.)

65. Kim, P., 'A Perspective on Brands', *Journal of Consumer Marketing*, v.7(3), autumn 1990, pp.63-67.

66. King, S., *Advertising as a Barrier to Market Entry*, Advertising Association, 1980.

67. King, S., 'Practical Progress from a Theory of Advertisements', *Admap*, v.11(10), October 1975, pp.338-343.

68. Klein, P.R., 'Evaluation vs. Diagnostic: Do You Have to Make a Choice?', Paper given at the 8th Annual ARF Copy Research Workshop – Copy Research: the New Evidence, New York, Advertising Research Foundation, September 1991.

69. Kover, A.J., 'What Gets Through? An Application of Post Modernist Media Theory to Advertising Research', Paper given at the 8th Annual ARF Copy Research Workshop – Copy Research: the New Evidence, New York, Advertising Research Foundation, 1991.

70 Krugman, H.E., 'Memory Without Recall, Exposure Without Perception', *Journal of Advertising Research*, v.17(4), August 1977, pp.7-12.

71. Krugman, H.E., 'Processes Underlying Exposure to Advertising', *American Psychologist*, v.23(4), April 1968, pp.245-253.

72.   Krugman, H.E., 'The Impact of Television Advertising: Learning without Involvement', *Public Opinion Quarterly*, v.29(3), autumn 1965, pp.349-356.

73.   Krugman, H.E., 'Why Three Exposures May Be Enough', *Journal of Advertising Research*, v.12(6), December 1972, pp.11-14.

74.   Lambin, J-J., *Advertising, Competition and Market Conduct in Oligopoly Over Time*, New York, American Elsevier, Oxford, North Holland Publishing Co., 1976.

75.   Lambin, J-J., 'What is the Real Impact of Advertising?', *Harvard Business Review*, v.53(3), May-June 1975, pp.139-147.

76.   Lannon, J. & Cooper, P., 'Humanistic Advertising: a Holistic Cultural Perspective', *International Journal of Advertising*, v.2(3), July-September 1983, pp.195-213.

77.   Leman, G., 'Sales, Saleability and the Saleability Gap', British Bureau of Television Advertising, 1969.

78.   Litzenroth, H., 'A Small Town in Germany: Single-source Data from a Controlled Micromarket', *Admap*, v.26(5), No.307, May 1991, pp.23-27.

79.   Lodish, L.M., 'The *How Advertising Works* Project: New Knowledge About Key Factors That Affect Television Advertising's Ability to Increase Brand Sales', Paper given at ARF Seminar – Breakthrough Marketplace Advertising Research for Bottom Line Results, New York, Advertising Research Foundation, November 1991.

80.   Lubetkin, B., 'Additional Major Findings from the *How Advertising Works* Study', Paper given at the ARF Seminar – Breakthrough Marketplace Research for Bottom Line Results, New York, Advertising Research Foundation, November 1991.

81. McDonald, C., 'Advertising Effectiveness Revisited', *Admap*, v.22(4), No.251, April 1986, pp.191-203.

82. McDonald, C., 'Myths, Evidence and Evaluation', *Admap*, v.16(11), November 1980, pp.546-555.

83. McDonald, C., 'What is the Short-term Effect of Advertising?', *Admap*, v.6(10), November 1970 pp.350-356, 366. (Also In *Market Researchers Look at Advertising. A Collection of ESOMAR Papers 1949-1979*, (Ed) Broadbent, S. pp.39-50, Sigmatext, 1980.) (Also In Naples, M.J., *Effective Frequency: The Relationship Between Frequency and Advertising Effectiveness,* pp.83-103, New York, Association of National Advertisers, 1979.)

84. McQueen, J., 'Important Learning About How Advertising Works in Stimulating Long-term Brand Growth', Paper given at the ARF Seminar – Breakthrough Marketplace Advertising Research for Bottom Line Results, New York, Advertising Research Foundation, 1991.

85. Naples, M.J., *Effective Frequency: the Relationship Between Frequency and Advertising Effectiveness,* New York, Association of National Advertisers, 1979.

86. Nelson, R., 'We Need Better Advertising More Than We Need Better Validity', Paper given at the 8th Annual ARF Copy Research Workshop – Copy Research: the New Evidence, New York, Advertising Research Foundation, September 1991.

87. Nielsen Marketing Research, Brochure describing HomeScan, US, Nielsen, 1991.

88. Ogilvy Centre for Research and Development, 'The Impact of Advertising Expenditures on Profits for Consumer Businesses', San Francisco, California: Ogilvy Centre forResearch and Development, June 1987.

89.   Oherlihy, C., 'Why Econometrics Can make Advertising and Marketing Scientific. A Reply to Tom Corlett', *Admap*, v.14(10), October 1978, pp.472-480. (NB. There are many more articles by Oherlihy on various aspects of econometrics in *Admap* from 1976 to 1986)

90.   Partnership for a Drug Free America, 'Attitudes Change', In *It Works! How Investment Spending in Advertising Pays Off*, Ryan, B., pp.31-37, New York, American Association of Advertising Agencies, 1991.

91.   Popper, K., *Unended Quest: an Intellectual Autobiography*, Fontana/Collins, 1976. (see chapter on Darwinism as Metaphysics, pp.167-180.)

92.   Prentice, R.M., 'A Breakthrough That Reveals Why Most Promotions Cost 7 Times as Much as Advertising', In *It Works! How Investment Spending in Advertising Pays Off*, Ryan, B., pp.19-21, New York, American Association of Advertising Agencies, 1991.

93.   Prue, T., 'Recall or Response? Ad Effectiveness Monitoring: the Real Issues', *Admap*, v.26(6), no.308, June 1991, pp.38-40.

94.   Reekie, W.D., *Advertising and Price*, Advertising Association, 1979.

95.   Roberts, A., 'The Decision Between Above- and Below-the-line', *Admap*, v.16(12), December 1980, pp.588-592.

96.   Schroer, J.C., 'Ad Spending: Growing Market Share', *Harvard Business Review*, v.68(1), January-February 1990, pp11-17.

97.   Simon, J.L., 'The Effect of Advertising upon the Propensity to Consume', In *Issues in the Economics of Advertising*, pp.193-217, Urbana, Illinois, University Illinois Press, 1970.

98.   Simon, J.L. & Arndt, J., 'The Shape of the Advertising Response Function', *Journal of Advertising Research*, v.20(4), August 1980, pp.11-28.

99.   Smith, A., 'Understanding More About the Way People Respond to Advertising Pressure', *Admap*, v.16(4), April 1980.

100. Spaeth, J. & Feldman, G., 'Integrating Evaluative and Diagnostic Measures: Know More About How Your Advertising Works', Paper given at the 8th Annual ARF Copy Research Workshop – Copy Research: the New Evidence, New York, Advertising Research Foundation, September 1991.

101. Starch, D., *Principles of Advertising*, Shaw, 1925.

102. Steiner, R.L., 'Does Advertising Lower Consumer Prices?', *Journal of Marketing*, v.37(4), October 1973, pp.19-27.

103. Stewart, M.J., 'The Long Term Effects of Econometrics', *Admap*, v.14(2), February 1978, pp64-70.

104. Thorson, E., 'Likeability: 10 Years of Academic Research', Paper given at the 8th Annual ARF Copy Research Workshop – Copy Research: the New Evidence, New York, Advertising Research Foundation, September 1991.

105. Vaughn, D., 'How Advertising Works: a Planning Model', *Journal of Advertising Research*, v.20(5), October, 1980, pp.27-33. (see also Berger, D. ref. 6)

106. Vaughn, D., 'How Advertising Works: a Planning Model Revisited', *Journal of Advertising Research*, v.26(1), February-March 1986, pp.57-66, (see also Berger, D. ref. 6)

107. Waterson, M.J., *Advertising, Brands and Markets*, Advertising Association, 1984

108. Young, J.W., *How to Become an Advertising Man*, Chicago, Advertising Publications Inc., 1963.

109. Zielske, H. A., 'The Remembering and Forgetting of Advertising', Journal of Marketing, V.23(1), January 1959.